HEROES OF HISTORY

DOUGLAS MACARTHUR

What Greater Honor

HEROES OF HISTORY

DOUGLAS MACARTHUR

What Greater Honor

JANET & GEOFF BENGE

Emerald Books

P.O. BOX 635, LYNNWOOD, WA 98046

Emerald Books are distributed through YWAM Publishing. For a full list of titles, including other great biographies, visit our website at www.ywampublishing.com or call 1-800-922-2143.

Douglas MacArthur: What Greater Honor
Copyright © 2005 by Janet and Geoff Benge

Published by Emerald Books
P.O. Box 635
Lynnwood, Washington 98046

Library of Congress Cataloging-in-Publication Data
Benge, Janet, 1958–
  Douglas MacArthur : what greater honor / by Janet and Geoff Benge.
    p. cm. — (Heroes of history)
  Includes bibliographical references.
  ISBN 1-932096-15-9
  1. MacArthur, Douglas, 1880–1964—Juvenile literature.
2. Generals—United States—Biography—Juvenile literature.
3. United States. Army—Biography— Juvenile literature.
4. United States—History, Military—20th century—Juvenile literature. I. Benge, Geoff, 1954– II. Title.
  E745.M3B46 2005
  355'.0092—dc22   2004024219

ISBN-13: 978-1-932096-15-6
ISBN-10: 1-932096-15-9

Third printing 2019

Printed in the United States of America

HEROES OF HISTORY
Biographies

Abraham Lincoln
Alan Shepard
Ben Carson
Benjamin Franklin
Benjamin Rush
Billy Graham
Captain John Smith
Christopher Columbus
Clara Barton
Davy Crockett
Daniel Boone
Douglas MacArthur
Elizabeth Fry
Ernest Shackleton
George Washington
George Washington Carver
Harriet Tubman
John Adams
Laura Ingalls Wilder
Louis Zamperini
Meriwether Lewis
Milton Hershey
Orville Wright
Ronald Reagan
Theodore Roosevelt
Thomas Edison
William Bradford
William Penn
William Wilberforce

Available in paperback, e-book, and audiobook formats.
Unit Study Curriculum Guides are available for each biography.
www.emeraldbooks.com

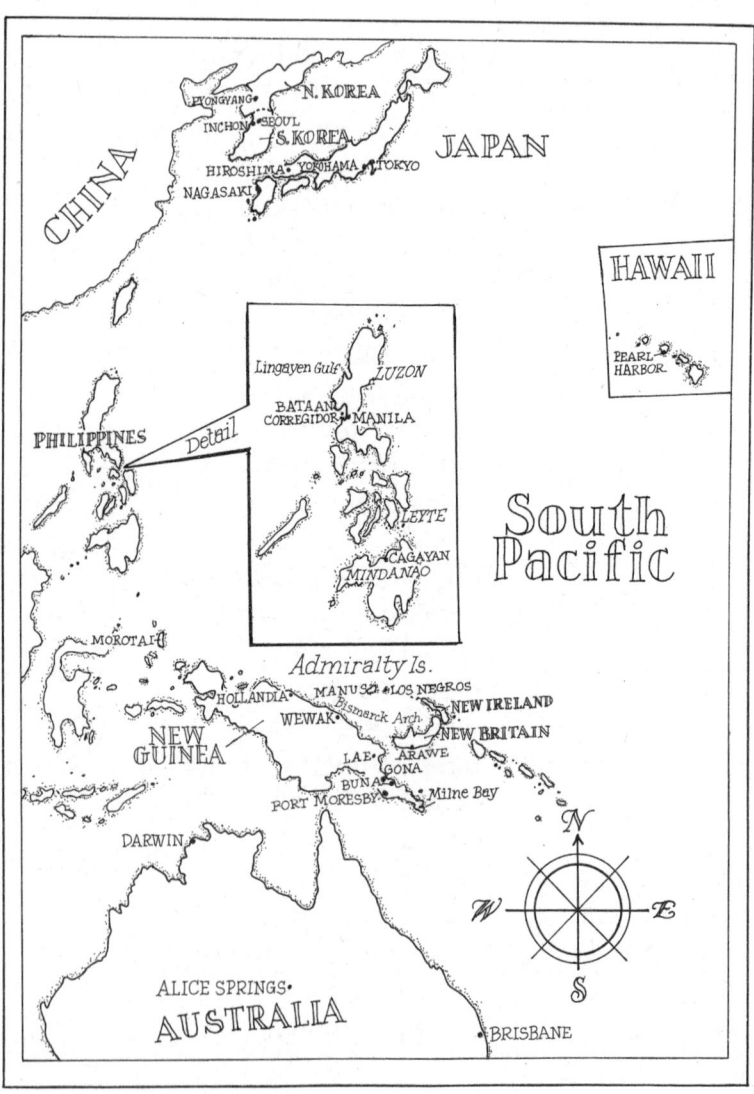

Contents

Chapter 1

He Would Return

The engine of the PT boat throbbed as Douglas MacArthur looked back at the outline of the island of Corregidor disappearing into the darkness. Douglas's wife and four-year-old son were sitting tensely beside him. Douglas sighed anxiously. The last thing he wanted to do was to leave now. Everything in him wanted to stay and fight till the death if it came to that. In fact, when the order had come for him to evacuate, his first impulse had been to resign his commission as commander in chief of the American armed forces in the Far East and volunteer to fight alongside the enlisted men. But his aides had talked him out of this. President Franklin Roosevelt and the Allies needed his military knowledge and experience to win the war. Why else, they asked, would the president have ordered Douglas to make such a perilous escape in order to assume the role of commander of the newly created theater of operations in the southwest Pacific region?

Begrudgingly Douglas accepted their argument, and now he was risking his life and the lives of his wife and son in a PT boat stealing away from the island fortress. He hoped that his officers knew that his heart was with them and the nine thousand American troops on Corregidor and the eighty thousand men valiantly fighting to hold back the Japanese on the Bataan peninsula beyond. Somehow, he promised himself, he would bring back reinforcements and rescue them. He would return!

The PT boat rendezvoused at a secretly designated location with the three other PT boats carrying members of Douglas's staff evacuating with him. The four boats formed a single line, then gingerly began to weave their way through the deadly minefield that guarded the entrance to the bay.

Douglas, who was never able to sit still for long, joined a crewman on the bow, and together they peered into the dark ocean, alert to any signs of the hidden mines.

As the boats idled along, they gave a false impression of safety and ease. Douglas knew full well the danger he and his family were in. One undetected mine and they would all be blown sky high. Despite that, this was probably the easiest leg of their journey. Beyond the minefield lay five hundred miles of open ocean—ocean that was enemy territory patrolled by Japanese naval vessels that would torpedo them on sight.

They were headed for Cagayan on the north coast of the southern Philippine island of Mindanao. It would be a heart-stopping trip, and when and if they got there, it was only the halfway point of the journey. From there Douglas would have to fly to his final destination, Australia, and once the Japanese learned he had escaped Corregidor, the sky would be filled with enemy fighters ready to shoot down his airplane.

Back on the island, he had calculated that they had only one chance in five of making it to their destination, but he had been ordered to make the dangerous journey, and he was doing his best to fulfill that order.

"Mine ahead," a lookout screamed, bringing Douglas's attention back to their present danger. Douglas had been getting too far ahead of himself. First they had to get through the minefield.

Suddenly the PT boat lurched to starboard, throwing Douglas off balance as the commander took immediate evasive action. The other boats followed his lead as they all continued to work their way through the deadly waters.

"We're all clear of the minefield, General," Douglas finally heard the boat commander announce after two harrowing hours. He gave a nod of gratitude as the big Packard engine opened up to full throttle, shaking the darkness.

As the PT boat smashed its way forward into the fifteen-foot waves of the open sea, Douglas thought how vast and different was the Pacific Ocean, in which the Philippines lay, from the West Texas desert that was home to his earliest memories. He recalled the army post outside El Paso where, as a five-year-old, he had gathered his first memories of reveille, parades, and practice maneuvers. Who could ever have imagined that from that dry, desolate place he would end up commanding forces spread across such a huge reach of ocean? As he had so many times before, Douglas wished his father were alive to see how far his youngest son had come.

Chapter 2

The Life of a Captain's Son

Douglas blinked and looked again. It was still there, a shaggy shape emerging from the sandy dunes around Fort Selden, near El Paso, Texas. Douglas pulled his spotted Navajo pony to a halt and shouted to his older brother. "Look, Arthur, over there. Do you think it's a camel?"

Douglas watched as his brother laughed and then turned in the direction he was pointing. Arthur glanced back at Douglas, his eyes wide. "It looks like it...it is a camel. But how could it be?" he mused. "Let's go and ask Father. He'll know what it is."

The two boys turned their horses and galloped back through the gates of the fort. They did not dismount until they were right in front of Captain Arthur MacArthur's office. Then they raced inside.

"Father, Father, you'll never guess what we saw," Douglas panted. "It was a camel. I'm sure it was a camel, about a mile outside the gate."

"Father, do you think we really saw one?" Arthur asked.

Captain MacArthur chuckled. "I think you did," he said. "And I bet I know where it came from. Back in the war, Jefferson Davis chartered a ship from Egypt to bring over herds of camels. He wanted them to be used as pack animals on the supply trains used to link the isolated forts in Indian country. Apparently they were stubborn, hard-to-manage creatures, and one by one they strayed off into the wilderness. You must have seen one of the survivors."

Although he was only five, Douglas knew that the war his father was referring to was the Civil War. His father had been a teenager when the war started, and Douglas was always thrilled to hear the stories his father told about meeting President Abraham Lincoln and his quick rise to the rank of regimental commander by the time he was eighteen and a half years old. How strange it was that now, in 1885, twenty years after the war had ended, some shaggy old camels were still wandering around Fort Selden, ghostly reminders of a bygone era.

"You boys coming?" a soldier yelled in the window as he walked by Captain MacArthur's office.

"Oh, yes," Douglas replied, looking at the clock on his father's wall. It was four o'clock. "We'll be back soon," he said as he and Arthur dashed for the door.

Two minutes later the two boys were sitting on a mule-drawn water wagon as it made its regular one-and-a-half-mile trip from Fort Selden to the Rio Grande. At the river the soldiers hand-pumped water into the large tank on the wagon, enough water to last those stationed at the fort for twenty-four hours.

Hitching a ride on the water wagon was one of Douglas's favorite activities. He never knew what he would see along the way. Normally it was not anything as startling as a camel; more often it was coyotes and sometimes Indians off in the distance.

In the evening Douglas always told his parents what he had seen during the day, and often his mother, Pinky MacArthur, made him write a few sentences about what he had seen when she tutored him in the morning.

Douglas had a wonderful life at Fort Selden. A hint of adventure was always in the air, especially when officers visited from the cavalry post at Fort Stanton to the east. That fort guarded the Mescalero Apache Indian reservation, and occasionally the two forts would get together to prepare for Indian raids, though Douglas could not recall one ever taking place.

One night in late 1886, Douglas returned from the nightly retreat and lowering of the flag ceremony to find his mother packing clothes into a trunk.

"Are we going to Norfolk?" he asked. His mother was from there, and about once a year she took the two boys back to Riveredge, the Hardy family estate at the foot of the bridge across the river at

Norfolk, Virginia. She had grown up in a mansion, and many of her nine brothers and sisters still lived in the area.

Pinky MacArthur smiled at Douglas. "Something better than that!" she exclaimed. "I expect everyone will know by tomorrow, so I might as well tell you. All of Company K has been relocated to Fort Leavenworth."

Douglas smiled because his mother looked so happy, but inside he was confused. "Where is that?" he finally asked.

"Only twenty miles or so from Kansas City. Can you imagine that? We will be less than a morning's ride away from civilization! And Fort Leavenworth is huge! Your father tells me there is a school there, and there'll be lots of children for you to play with."

Douglas gulped. It was great news—he supposed—although he needed time to think about all of the things he would be leaving behind here near the Texas border with Mexico.

That night Douglas's mother came to tuck him into bed as usual. Douglas had a million questions he wanted to ask her, but he kept silent.

"Good night," his mother said. "And don't forget. You must grow up to be a great man like Robert E. Lee."

Douglas nodded. His mother always said the same thing to him at bedtime. And although he knew Robert E. Lee had fought for the South in the Civil War and his father had fought for the North, it did not seem strange to him that his mother always made Robert E. Lee out to be a hero. To her, war was all about bravery and duty, no matter which side of a conflict a soldier was on.

After his mother left, Douglas lay awake in bed for a long time. When the moon came up, he got out of bed and stood by the window, looking out at the parade ground he knew so well. Each twilight for as long as Douglas could remember, he and Arthur had stood at attention watching the retreat ceremony and listening as the bugle sounded for the lowering of the flag. Beyond the parade ground sat a single-story, flat-roof adobe building that served as the enlisted men's barracks.

Fort Selden was the only home Douglas could remember, although he knew that he had been born at the army fort in Little Rock, Arkansas, and that soon after his arrival, his father had been assigned to Fort Wingate in New Mexico. The MacArthur family had lived there until Douglas was four years old. It was not a time his father or mother talked about much. During their stay at Fort Wingate, five-year-old Malcolm MacArthur, their middle son, had died of measles. Douglas, who was three at the time, did not remember his older brother's life or his death.

For Douglas, the life he could recall revolved around the army at Fort Selden. His father was a captain and in command of forty-six enlisted men. Douglas knew each man under his father's command well, and many of the men treated him and Arthur like their own sons.

As he thought about the move, Douglas wondered what it would be like at Fort Leavenworth. His mother had told him that all of Company K was moving, which meant that his best friend Billy Hughes, the son of Company K's junior officer, would be going with them. At least together, Douglas decided, he and Billy could face anything, even school.

When the long trip north began, Douglas, Arthur, and Billy were all eager for the adventure. Although railway tracks now stretched from Baltimore to San Francisco, no tracks were nearby, and Company K had to make the trip to Fort Leavenworth, Kansas, on wagons and carts. Apache Indians occasionally swooped down through the mountains and attacked white settlers, so the boys were constantly on the lookout for horses on the horizon. But they did not see any, and the trek north went smoothly.

From the moment they marched into Fort Leavenworth, Douglas missed the carefree life at Fort Selden. He was put into second grade, where he found the work easy but boring. His father was no longer the highest-ranking officer, and Douglas often heard his mother encouraging his father not to give up hope that he would be promoted soon.

It seemed like a long shot. Douglas's father was forty-one years old and had remained a captain for twenty-two years, having been overlooked for many promotions. Douglas could not understand why this was. His father was certainly one of the bravest men he knew. He had received the Medal of Honor for bravery during the Civil War, following the Battle of Missionary Ridge in 1863. He even kept a wad of letters with a bullet imbedded in them. The letters had been in the breast pocket of his uniform when a Confederate bullet struck him in the chest.

The wad of paper had stopped the bullet from piercing his heart and killing him.

Finally, in the summer of 1889, a vacancy came up in the adjutant general's office in Washington, D.C. This time Douglas could tell that his mother had her sights set on his father getting the position. She stood over his father while he wrote letters asking old army friends for recommendations. Before long, letters of recommendation were flowing in, including one that his mother insisted on reading aloud at dinner.

"Listen to this, boys," she said, her eyes shining with delight. "It's from Major General McCook, and this is what he says about your father: 'He is beyond question the most distinguished Captain in the army of the U.S. for gallantry and good conduct in war. He is a student, a master of his profession, has legal ability, which fits him for the position he seeks, is exceptional in habit, temperate at all times, yet modest withal.' If that doesn't get your father the promotion, I don't know what will!" she exclaimed.

Sure enough, in midsummer Captain MacArthur received the good news that he had been promoted to the rank of major and transferred to Washington, D.C. Once again Douglas, who was nine years old by then, had mixed feelings about the move, and once again his mother was enthusiastic about what lay ahead. "Just think of it, Douglas," she told him. "If you work hard at school, I'm certain you could get into West Point Academy."

Douglas was not sure whether that sounded like a good idea, but by now he knew better than to interfere with his mother's plans. If she wanted him to get into West Point, he had no doubt that he would end up there.

Once they got to Washington, Douglas adjusted to the family's new home on Rhode Island Avenue. It was close to Force Public School, where his mother enrolled him.

The best thing about the move to Washington for Douglas was that he got to spend time with his seventy-four-year-old Yankee grandfather, who, like his brother and father, was named Arthur MacArthur. His grandfather told wonderful stories about emigrating from Scotland as a child aboard one of the first steamships. Once he had settled in America, he put himself through law school and began a long and distinguished career as a lawyer and then judge. He was even governor of Wisconsin for six days, the result of a complicated legal situation Douglas did not fully understand.

In Washington, D.C., the days of Douglas and his brother watching artillery practice or the cavalry parade were gone. Now his father went to work in a large office wearing his dress uniform. Douglas did his best to adjust to the pomp and ceremony of his father's new job, but he did not enjoy it.

In school Douglas's mind often drifted back to the freedom and spare time he had enjoyed as a captain's son at Fort Selden. School was a trial to Douglas, and although his mother nagged him, he seldom got better than a C grade. His brother Arthur fared much better at school, earning straight A's and inspiring the MacArthurs to do all they could to get their oldest son into West Point. Despite a flurry of letter writing and visits to an array of governors, senators, congressmen, and bishops, Arthur did not win a place at West Point and instead had to be content with attending the Naval Academy at Annapolis, Maryland.

In the fall of 1893, a year after Arthur had entered the naval academy, Douglas's father brought home some startling news—he had been transferred from Washington, D.C., to San Antonio, Texas.

From the moment he heard the news, Douglas was jubilant. Fort Sam Houston was one of the largest and most important forts the army maintained. Its garrison guarded the southern border with Mexico against smugglers, and Douglas's imagination soared with thoughts of riding along as the troops patrolled the border and of hunting wild game.

It did not take Douglas long to realize that this time his mother was not enthusiastic about the move. She loved the pageantry and formality of living in the nation's capital, and it took the promise of frequent trips home to Virginia and a live-in maid to brighten her outlook on the move.

The only good news about the transfer, she told Douglas, was that a new high school had just been opened at the fort. It was called the West Texas Military Academy, and Douglas had already been enrolled there.

For the first time ever, the MacArthur family journeyed to their new posting by train. Thirteen-year-old Douglas was almost as excited about the fifteen-hundred-mile train ride as he was about the new adventures awaiting him in Texas.

Chapter 3

A Determined
Young Man

Douglas whistled as the train pulled up at the station outside Fort Sam Houston, the biggest army garrison he had ever seen. Soon eager hands were reaching for their luggage, and the three MacArthurs were being escorted to their new living quarters.

The following morning Douglas dressed in his braided gray cadet uniform. Then at 8:10 he made his way across the lower parade ground of Fort Sam, as the garrison was referred to by most, to the school chapel. Other boys were strolling the same way, and Douglas smiled shyly at several of them. The boys who boarded at the institute marched into the chapel just ahead of him, and then all of the boys took their seats for the morning chapel service.

When the service was over, the school day began, and by lunchtime Douglas had noticed that some very rough boys were in his classes. He soon learned that many of these rough boys had been in trouble and were sent to the West Texas Military Academy to be reformed. Everyone knew that Douglas was the new kid in the fort and that his father was the new major of the corps. As a result, hardly anyone was willing to reach out and be his friend.

Instead of worrying about this, Douglas determined that he was going to be the best student he could be. For the first time in his life he took his studies seriously, listening intently to the teachers and making sure that he did even more homework than was required.

Within weeks he was getting better grades than ever before. And much to his surprise, Douglas found that he enjoyed the challenge of getting good grades. He especially liked learning Latin and Greek, because he could read some of the greatest speeches of all times in their original language.

By the end of his first year in the school, Douglas was the top student in his class, as he was the following year as well. By his third year he was one of the most popular boys in school. This was mostly due to his being a junior and able to play on the institute's top sports teams. What Douglas lacked in natural athletic talent he made up for in sheer stamina and determination. By his senior year Douglas was quarterback on the football team and a swift shortstop on the baseball team. Both of these teams went undefeated, enhancing Douglas's popularity even more. He was also the best tennis player at the fort, and he won the speech competition. These achievements made his parents extremely proud. They were even happier when he graduated with a ninety-seven-point grade average and won a host of medals and prizes for his efforts in sports and academics.

Pinky MacArthur was particularly pleased with her son's achievements. She was still determined that Douglas would attend West Point and reminded him that he needed those excellent grades. Douglas's only regret was that his grandfather MacArthur had died the year before and was unable to see how well he had done.

By the time he graduated as the valedictorian of the class of 1897 at age seventeen, Douglas knew that deep down he wanted to attend West Point, not for his parents' sake but because he had made up his mind to become a soldier. He had the grades to qualify for entrance to West Point, but when he went for a preliminary physical examination, he received shocking news. The doctor informed Douglas that he had curvature of the spine and was medically unfit to enter West Point.

Douglas was flabbergasted by this news; after all, his sports record was excellent. He hardly knew what to think about his future, but his mother knew just what to do—a medical problem would not keep her son out of West Point, not if there was any way to cure it. She encouraged Douglas not to give up and made an appointment for him to see

Dr. Franz Pfister, a well-respected surgeon in Milwaukee, Wisconsin.

Dr. Pfister told Douglas that there was a possibility that he could cure his spinal problem, as long as Douglas was prepared to do special exercises every day and follow all of his instructions for one year. Douglas jumped at the opportunity and made plans to move to Milwaukee. At the same time, his father received a new appointment to St. Paul, Minnesota. While his father went to St. Paul, his mother went to Milwaukee to help Douglas with his therapy. Douglas's father promised to join them on the weekends.

By October 1897 Douglas and his mother were living at Plankinton House, an exclusive hotel, and the rehabilitation work on the spinal condition had begun. Douglas worked with Dr. Pfister every day, stretching and twisting his back muscles and lifting heavy weights. While he was at the clinic, his mother paid visits to many important men in town, asking for letters recommending Douglas for next year's intake of cadets to West Point.

The most influential man Pinky MacArthur visited was Congressman Theabold Otjen. To go to West Point as a cadet, one had to be sponsored by a member of the United States Senate or House of Representatives. Congressman Otjen had been a good friend of Douglas's grandfather and promised to sponsor Douglas if he did well enough in the entrance examination.

But for now Douglas had to help himself. Even when his muscles ached and his back felt like it could not stretch another inch, he kept up his daily exercise program. In addition, his mother enrolled him in classes at West End High so that he would not forget what he had learned at school the year before. The school was two miles from the hotel, and Douglas toughened himself up by walking there and back every day, even when it was snowing.

On April 25, 1898, while Douglas was still working with Dr. Pfister in Milwaukee and studying hard at school, Congress approved President McKinley's request for a declaration of war against Spain. Many newspapers, particularly those owned by William Randolph Hearst, had given much coverage to the appalling treatment of Cubans by the Spanish. As a result, public opinion had begun to grow in favor of annexing Spain's colonies, particularly those nearest to the United States. And when the American battleship *Maine* exploded and sank in Havana harbor on February 15, 1898, the clamor for war had grown even greater, until Congress felt compelled to act.

When Douglas read about the declaration of war, he wanted desperately to go and fight. He was even more determined to sign up for military service when he learned that his older brother Arthur had been deployed aboard a naval vessel that was part of Admiral Dewey's fleet. Arthur wrote enthusiastically about how he was headed for the Philippines, the Spanish colony located in the far reaches of the western Pacific Ocean, off the mainland of Southeast Asia. But Douglas's father discouraged him from signing up to serve, explaining that there would be other wars that he could fight in and that the most important thing for him right then was to concentrate on getting into West Point.

In early May Douglas read in the newspaper of Admiral Dewey's stunning victory in the Philippines. Dewey, having steamed quickly across the Pacific, had slipped into Manila Bay on May 1 and destroyed the Spanish fleet anchored there.

On June 1, 1898, a telegram arrived at Plankinton House addressed to Douglas and his mother. Pinky MacArthur slipped the telegram out of its envelope and read it aloud to her son. Douglas's chest puffed out when he learned that his father had been promoted to the rank of brigadier general. "I have been confirmed and commission signed by President. Secretary war directs me report immediately General Merritt San Francisco for duty expedition for Philippines," the rest of the telegram read.

While Douglas would have loved to march off to war in the Philippines with his father, it was time for him to take the entrance examination for West Point. For the first time in his life Douglas was so nervous that he could not sleep. By breakfast he felt sick to his stomach and wondered how he could possibly take the exam. He told his mother how he felt, and she accompanied him to City Hall, where the examination was to be held.

Before they walked up the steps to City Hall, Douglas stopped and looked pleadingly at his mother, hoping she would give him permission to go home. But Pinky MacArthur just put her hands firmly on her son's shoulders and looked into his eyes. "Doug, you'll win if you don't lose your nerve," she said. "You must believe in yourself, my son, or no one else will believe in you. Be self-confident, self-reliant, and even if you don't make it, you will know you have done your best." Then she smiled at him and pointed to the double doors. "Now go and do it," she said.

Douglas straightened himself up. He felt much better. He knew his mother was right. He had been working so hard to get into West Point, and all he had to do was to keep believing that he could make it.

With that he strode up the stairs, found his way to the examination room, and sat down with the other twelve applicants from the area who were taking the examination.

On June 7, 1898, the *Milwaukee Journal* carried the results of the West Point entrance examination. Douglas caught a glimpse of the headline as he returned to Plankinton House that night. The headline read, "He Will Go To West Point." Reading the next line, Douglas realized that the "he" in the headline was him! He quickly bought the newspaper and hurried upstairs to show his mother, who stood waiting for him inside their room, clutching a copy of the newspaper herself.

"Isn't it wonderful!" Pinky MacArthur exclaimed. "See what believing in yourself and hard work can do for you. Oh, listen to what it says." She began to read aloud from the newspaper:

> Young MacArthur is a remarkably bright, clever, and determined boy. His standing was 99 $\frac{1}{3}$ against the next man's 77.9. He

scored 700 points out of a possible 750. He is eighteen years old and resides with his mother in the Plankinton House. He came to the examinations with the determination to win after studying very hard in preparation for the tests and gave the strictest attention while at work, and consequently, like Dewey and Hobson, put aside all possibility of failure in his undertaking. He accomplished his purpose with a big margin to spare.

The newspaper article, however, did not account for one thing: Douglas still had to retake his medical exam.

The physical examination left Douglas deeply disappointed. The doctor who conducted the exam said that while he saw a great improvement, Douglas's back still was not straight enough to pass.

That afternoon Douglas took a long walk in the country. At first he was angry that his back was not straight enough, especially since he had worked so hard and done everything Dr. Pfister told him to. But as he walked, he calmed down and asked himself what he really wanted to do with his life now. He tried to imagine himself as a lawyer like his grandfather, or a politician or farmer, but he could not. Somehow he was sure his destiny lay as an officer in the army. *So I didn't make it this year,* Douglas told himself, *but the good news is that the exercises are working and my back is getting straighter. If I work twice as hard this year, I bet I can get into the next class.*

When he got back to Plankinton House, Douglas learned that his mother had already been to see Congressman Otjen, and because of Douglas's excellent marks in the written exam, the congressman was prepared to hold the opening for Douglas at West Point for one year. Douglas was relieved. *Things are going to work out after all,* he told himself.

Douglas once again threw himself into Dr. Pfister's exercise regime. As he worked at overcoming the curvature of his spine, he kept himself informed from the newspaper and letters from his father about what was happening in the Philippines. There had been so much publicity about Theodore Roosevelt and his Rough Riders overrunning the Spanish at San Juan Hill in Cuba that Douglas had to search for information about the Philippines. He was rewarded with articles that reported that his father, Brigadier General Arthur MacArthur, had arrived in the Philippines on July 31, 1898, and had been given command of the 1st Brigade of General Merritt's 8th Army Corps.

The articles also reported that as a result of the defeat of the Spanish fleet, thirty-five thousand Spanish soldiers were trapped in Manila with no way of escape. The only course of action left to them was to fight. Two weeks after his arrival, Douglas's father led his brigade in an attack to capture Manila and rout these Spanish soldiers. Brigadier General MacArthur's men encountered stiff resistance, and a number of the men were killed or wounded in the battle. Despite the fierce fighting, the Spanish were subdued, and the American forces quickly captured the city. General Merritt placed the city under martial law, and Douglas's father was made provost marshal, charged with maintaining the peace in Manila.

Douglas was proud as he read in the newspaper of his father's military achievements and dreamed of the day when he, too, might take part in some great campaign like the battle for Manila.

In December 1898 a peace conference was held in Paris, where the United States agreed to pay Spain twenty million dollars to annex the Philippine Islands. As part of the peace agreement, the United States also took control of the former Spanish colonies of Guam and Puerto Rico.

Although the Spanish-American War was officially over, Douglas soon learned that his father was involved in more fighting in the Philippines. Many Filipinos were outraged when they learned that the United States had taken control of their country. They banded together under the leadership of Emilio Aguinaldo and revolted, declaring the country independent. Once again Brigadier General MacArthur was ordered into combat, this time to stop the Filipino rebellion. This fight was not as swift as the battle for Manila had been, but Douglas's father soon managed to push the rebels away from the major cities and into the mountains and outlying islands. By February 1899 the headlines in the newspapers in the United States declared, "'Tis Dewey on the Sea, and MacArthur on the Land."

Once again Douglas's chest puffed out with pride at his father's exploits on the battlefield.

Although he was proud of his father, Douglas did not lose sight of his own goal. He continued to pour every ounce of his energy into passing his physical examination and getting into West Point. And his efforts paid off. In May 1899 he passed his physical and was accepted into West Point. It had taken two years longer to get there than he would have liked, but that didn't matter now. What mattered was that nineteen-year-old Douglas MacArthur was off to West Point.

Chapter 4

An Officer in Training

Sunlight streamed into the carriage as the train puffed its way up the Hudson River Valley on June 13, 1899. Douglas sat peering out the window. He felt sure that he must be the happiest young man in America. He was much too excited to read. After two years of hard work, he was finally on his way to West Point and, he hoped, to a distinguished career just like his father's. By now Brigadier General Arthur MacArthur, Admiral George Dewey, and Teddy Roosevelt were the three most celebrated military figures in the United States, and Douglas knew he had big shoes to fill. He could hardly wait to get started.

There was just one possible problem: Douglas's mother was sitting right beside him, clad in her black twill traveling dress. Pinky MacArthur was not just accompanying Douglas to West Point to help him settle in, she was coming to stay! She had already booked herself into Craney's Hotel, located just outside the gates to the military academy, and she planned to stay there for the entire four years Douglas would be in training.

Douglas tried not to pay too much attention to how this would look. It was hard to imagine that the other boys would not label him a mama's boy, but there was nothing he could do about it. No matter how much he had protested, his mother insisted that she was coming along, and now here she was sitting right next to him.

Within a few minutes Douglas spotted the West Point station, a tan brick building with a steep tiled roof. A conductor passed through their carriage. "This is it, lad," he told Douglas. "Best of luck. I hope you are man enough to handle it."

"Thank you, sir," Douglas said, tipping the ten-gallon Stetson he had chosen to wear for his entrance into West Point.

With luggage in hand, Douglas and his mother made their way up the steep stone path, the academy towering above them. The path ended on a wide shelf of land overlooking the Hudson River. The two of them stopped to admire the breathtaking view of the waterway and then the various buildings that surrounded the shelf of land.

"Just think, Douglas. Some of these buildings are one hundred years old. I wonder which barracks Robert E. Lee lived in. Maybe you'll end up there. Wouldn't that be wonderful?" his mother exclaimed as the two of them walked toward the main entranceway. To the left of the entrance stood an antebellum building, Craney's Hotel.

"How perfect," Pinky MacArthur said. "Look, I'm only a few hundred feet away from where you will be. When we get the schedule, we can work out when you will come to visit me. Probably just before dinner will be best, and you must come every day, of course."

Douglas nodded, though he wondered whether it was possible to get a regular pass. Back in Milwaukee he had talked to a West Point graduate who told him that cadets were allowed off campus only a few times a year, to attend army-navy football games and for summer vacation at the end of the school year. They had no other days off, and they were on their honor not to dismount if they rode beyond the academy on horseback.

That evening Douglas and his mother were given a tour of West Point. Douglas was fascinated with the huge chain on Trophy Point. During the Revolutionary War the chain had been strung all the way across the Hudson River to stop British ships from sailing upriver.

The following morning Douglas was among the 332 cadets who gathered on the parade ground. The cadets were divided by class, and Douglas soon learned his first words of West Point jargon. The new cadets, like him, were called "plebes," the second-year cadets, "yearlings," the third-year cadets, "second classmen," and the fourth-year cadets, "first classmen." The best all-round first classman was called the "first captain," and he was the cadet leader of the entire group.

The current first captain explained to the plebes that they were going to spend their first three weeks at West Point in Beast Barracks, tents set up on Clinton Field on the other side of the parade ground. One evening as Douglas sat in his tent with his roommate Frederick Cunningham, a group of upperclassmen arrived and ordered Douglas to follow them. Douglas gulped, knowing this must be the dreaded hazing he had heard so much about. Obediently he followed the upperclassmen to their dorm, where he was ordered to straddle a pile of broken glass laid out in a bull's-eye shape on the floor. He was then ordered to do deep-knee bends, with his arms held straight out in front of him, making sure that his buttocks touched the back of his heels with each bend. This was known as "eagling," which, along with a variety of other initiation practices, was inflicted on the new recruits by the upperclassmen.

Douglas complied with their command. As he began doing deep-knee bends, the older students taunted him for having a father who was now a famous general and for having his mother living nearby at Craney's Hotel.

For forty minutes Douglas kept doing deep-knee bends. He wasn't quite sure how many he had done. He had lost count at 230, but he supposed he had probably done 250 by now. All of a sudden he began to feel weak. The room spun, and the abusive voices became a babble and then faded away. As he was about to descend into yet another knee bend, he felt himself tumble forward, and he crashed to the floor unconscious.

After several minutes on the floor, Douglas regained consciousness, and the upperclassmen ordered him to return to his tent. Somehow he stumbled back to the field and flopped down in his tent. As Frederick rushed to his roommate's aid, Douglas's body began to convulse violently. His feet beat uncontrollably against the wooden floor of the tent, and his arms flailed wildly. Despite his condition, Douglas was conscious enough to ask Frederick to put a blanket under his feet to dampen the noise on the floor. He was worried that an officer might hear the noise and come to investigate and find him in this condition. "And if I cry out," Douglas instructed his roommate, "put a blanket in my mouth to muffle the sound so I will not be heard."

The following morning when Douglas awoke, he was still lying on the floor where he had collapsed. The convulsions had stopped, but he felt wretched. His body, particularly his knees and thighs, and his head throbbed, and he felt like vomiting. He was thankful that when he fainted while being hazed, he had toppled forward. If he had fallen backward onto the jagged glass, his back and thighs would have been cut to ribbons.

"You should go and see the doctor," Frederick urged as Douglas struggled to his feet.

"No," Douglas replied. "What they did may well be cruel, but if it is what I must endure to take my place in this academy, then endure it I will." With that Douglas splashed some cold water on his face, straightened his uniform, and headed out to the parade ground, where he fell in line with the other new recruits for roll call.

After three weeks in the Beast Barracks, the hazing of the new recruits was finally over. The plebes were moved into regular rooms, and the academic year began in earnest.

As it happened, Douglas was able to get a pass to visit his mother for half an hour most evenings, and he often walked to Craney's Hotel with Ulysses S. Grant III. Ulysses was the grandson of Ulysses S. Grant, the famous Civil War Union general and former president of the United States. Ulysses' mother had also come to "supervise" her son's West Point education, and she, too, was staying at the hotel.

Douglas and his mother continued their intense interest in what was going on in the Philippines. In November the American government declared the rebellion there officially over. But Douglas's father had strongly objected to this move because Emilio Aguinaldo and his pro-independence fighters had not been destroyed. He did not think there could be lasting peace in the Philippines until the rebel army had been completely crushed.

During his second year at West Point, Douglas found himself drawn into an inquiry into hazing practices at the military academy. The year before Douglas had arrived at West Point, a plebe named Oscar Booz had been severely hazed. He had left the institution as a result of the ordeal, and a year and a half later he died of tuberculosis. His congressman blamed his death in part on the hazing, and as public pressure mounted, President McKinley ordered a special inquiry into hazing at West Point to be convened immediately.

Douglas was never quite sure how or why it happened, but he was called as a witness before the committee carrying out the inquiry. The situation put him in a quandary. He wanted to tell the truth, but at the same time he did not want to name the names of those who had mercilessly hazed him.

Before Douglas went to testify, his mother told him, "Never lie, never tattle." Douglas did his best to live by his mother's maxim as he carefully, with guarded words, answered the committee members' questions.

"Did you expect when you came to West Point to be treated in this manner?" Congressman Edmund Diggs of New York asked, beginning the questioning for the committee.

"Not exactly in that manner, no, sir," Douglas replied.

"Did you not consider it cruel at the time?" the congressman asked.

"I was perhaps surprised to some extent," Douglas replied.

"I wish you would answer my question. Did you or did you not consider it cruel at the time?" Congressman Diggs responded, becoming a little irritated.

Choosing his words carefully, Douglas said, "I would like to have you define cruel."

"All right, sir," the congressman began. "Disposed to inflict suffering, indifferent in the presence of suffering, hard-hearted, inflicting pain mentally or physically, causing suffering."

"I would say perhaps it was cruel, then," Douglas replied.

"You have qualified your answer. Was it or was it not cruel?" Congressman Diggs inquired.

"Yes, sir," Douglas admitted.

"And you did not expect it was part of the essential education of an officer to be subjected to such cruelty?" the congressman pressed.

"I do not think it is essential, no, sir," Douglas said.

"And do you believe that an army officer, or a man who may become an officer of the United States Army, should not treat one of his fellow officers, or someone who is going to be a fellow officer, in that cruel manner?"

"I should say not; no, sir," Douglas said forthrightly.

By considering the questions and carefully crafting his answers in this manner, Douglas made it through the inquiry. By the end of his questioning, Douglas was proud of his performance. He had followed his mother's advice: he had told the truth, and when pressed by the committee to name those he knew who had participated in hazing, he had repeated the names of the three cadets who had already been expelled from the academy for meting out cruel bouts of hazing.

With his part in the special inquiry into hazing practices now behind him, Douglas threw himself back into his studies. He found himself instantly popular because he had not named any names at the inquiry. Indeed, his performance before the committee had won him the lasting respect of the other cadets at West Point.

While the special inquiry had been taking place, Douglas learned that his father had been appointed the military governor of the Philippines. His father wrote to him, outlining many of the difficulties involved in his new posting. The rebels were still active and were hard to fight, especially now that the president had declared that the war was over in the Philippines. Another problem his father faced was dealing with the Philippine Commission, headed by William Taft, which the president had dispatched to the Philippines. It was often unclear who should make a particular decision, Douglas's father or Taft. The two men jockeyed for power, and then on July 4, 1901, Taft was sworn in as the civilian governor of the Philippines, responsible for reorganizing the national and municipal governments and reforming the police, judiciary, and tax system. Soon afterward Douglas's father wrote to say that he was leaving the Philippines to come home.

When Brigadier General Arthur MacArthur finally made it to West Point to visit his wife and son, Douglas had great news for him. Not only was he now a second-year cadet, but also he had completed his first year at West Point with the top grades in his class.

Over the summer the MacArthur family enjoyed a wonderful time together, and Arthur, Douglas's brother, announced that he planned to marry his girlfriend, Mary McCulla, early in 1902. Mary's father had served with Brigadier General MacArthur in the Philippines, and both families thought the marriage was a splendid match.

When Douglas returned to West Point after the summer, the first thing he did was request special leave to attend the wedding. Everything went well, but when Douglas suggested that he might get married when he graduated, his mother quickly reminded him that he was already married to his army career and that he must not let anything—or anyone—interfere with that.

Chapter 5

Lieutenant Douglas MacArthur

Under the watchful eye of his mother, Douglas continued to study hard at West Point. During his third year he again received top academic honors, as well as winning his letter *A* in baseball. Best of all, he was appointed first captain of the corps for the following year. This was a great honor, and Douglas wired his father immediately to tell him of the good news. His mother was especially delighted, as Douglas was following in the footsteps of her Civil War hero Robert E. Lee, who had been first captain in 1829.

The gold stripes of first captain carried with them a lot of responsibilities. Douglas served as the representative of the superintendent, the head of West Point, inspected the mess hall, and gave the command for the cadets to retire every evening.

As expected, Douglas carried out these duties well, and when it was time to graduate, he had the highest marks of any cadet in the past twenty-five years at West Point.

On Thursday, June 11, 1903, Douglas MacArthur and the fellow cadets in his class became members of the Long Grey Line, as graduates of West Point were called. Douglas's father and mother were invited to sit on the platform with the other important guests at the graduation, but they chose to sit in the audience behind the graduating class, among the parents and relatives of the other graduating cadets.

When the processional music began, Douglas led the line of ninety-three graduates from their seats up to the platform. After he saluted and accepted his diploma, there was an outburst of applause. On the spur of the moment, Douglas turned quickly, and instead of returning to his seat, he marched down the aisle to where his parents sat. With tears in his eyes he handed the diploma to his father and smiled at his mother. Then he returned to his seat. It was a moment he knew he would never forget.

Secretary of War Elihu Root gave the commencement address, concluding his speech with the words, "Before you leave the army, according to all precedent in our history, you will be engaged in another war. It is bound to come, and will come. Prepare your country for that war."

Douglas took the secretary's words to heart.

On September 23, 1903, Lieutenant Douglas MacArthur stood on the aft deck of the transport ship *Sherman* bound for Manila, the Philippines. He could not have been more pleased with the way things had turned out in the weeks following his graduation from West Point. As the top graduate, he had been given the choice of which branch of the army he wanted to enter, and he had chosen the Corps of Engineers. It was widely accepted that the smartest and the brightest cadets went into the corps because it offered the fastest track to promotion. Better still, Douglas had been assigned to the Philippines, where American troops could possibly see action in 1903.

In his spare time on the thirty-eight-day voyage across the Pacific Ocean, Douglas studied a map of the Philippine Islands. There were 7,083 of them, stretching from the same latitude as China's Hainan island all the way down to Indonesia. As the *Sherman* steamed into Manila Bay, Douglas thought of his father arriving there five years before and valiantly leading his men in the fight to capture the city from the Spanish. Douglas also discovered that, as his father had predicted, the Americans in the Philippines still faced many challenges, particularly from the Filipino rebel forces still active in the mountainous regions and outlying islands.

Douglas's first assignment in the Philippines with the Corps of Engineers was twofold. He was to supervise the construction of a dock in Tacloban on the island of Leyte while leading patrols that were on the lookout for rebels operating in the area. As Douglas soon found out, the first task involved a lot of hard work, and the second nearly proved fatal.

It was mid-November, and Douglas was leading a group of soldiers out into the dense tropical jungle of Leyte. As they made their way, they heard a rustle among the foliage. Douglas turned in the direction of the noise. Suddenly he heard a bullet crack through the thick, humid air and embed itself in the trunk of a tree behind him. He was shocked to realize that the bullet had first passed through the peak of his cap. As he dropped to the ground for cover, Douglas reached for his .38-caliber pistol and shot at the two rebel guerrillas now clearly visible amid the jungle. His bullets struck and instantly killed both men.

One of Douglas's men, an Irish sergeant, raced forward to make sure the two rebels were dead. Then he turned and looked at the gaping bullet hole in Douglas's cap. "Beggin' the lieutenant's pardon," he said respectfully, "but all the rest of the lieutenant's life is pure velvet."

Douglas, his face ashen, was too shaken to reply. But with bravado after the incident, he wrote to his mother, "I heard the bullets whistle, and believe me, there is something charming in the sound."

This incident, along with the MacArthur name, made Douglas an instant hero in the area.

Douglas was not able to stay on Leyte for long, however. In January 1904 he came down with a bad case of malaria and had to be transferred to an army hospital in Manila. It was a bitter pill to swallow, and he fought hard to rehabilitate himself as fast as possible.

One good thing that Douglas discovered about being back in Manila was that he was able to keep up with the latest world news. In 1894–95, in a short war known as the Sino-Japanese War, Japan had ended China's political influence over Korea and had begun to exert its own influence over the Korean peninsula. Soon afterward Russia had begun to exert its influence over the Chinese province of Manchuria to the north of Korea, and a military standoff between the Japanese and the Russians had begun. Finally, in February 1904, as Douglas lay in the hospital still sick with malaria, he read how Japanese troops had landed in Korea and moved north into Manchuria to confront the Russians. Then in April he read how the Japanese navy had destroyed the Russian Pacific fleet at Port Arthur, Manchuria. As tensions mounted between the two countries, the United States kept a watchful eye on the situation.

After his recovery Douglas passed the examination to become a first lieutenant. His first assignment with his new rank was to survey the harbor at Mariveles at the tip of the Bataan peninsula, across Manila Bay. When he had completed this job and returned to Manila, Douglas was devastated to learn that he was being reassigned back to San Francisco. The Corps of Engineers was becoming increasingly involved in government engineering projects, and a team was needed to survey some valleys in California. To make matters worse, Douglas learned that his father was in Manchuria as an observer of what was now being called the Russo-Japanese War. Douglas would have given anything to join his father, but he was under orders to return to the United States, and he could do nothing about it.

When he arrived back in San Francisco, Douglas found his mother frantic. She was worried about his father and was not coping well with being alone. Douglas tried to help her, but he suffered a relapse of malaria and spent the next several weeks lying in bed.

After his recovery Douglas spent the next year working with the Corps of Engineers in the San Francisco area, until he received a telegram on October 3, 1905:

Special Order War Department
No. 222 Washington, D.C.
October 3, 1905

First Lieutenant Douglas MacArthur, corps of engineers, is relieved from present duties, and will proceed to Tokyo, Japan, and report in person to Major General Arthur MacArthur, U.S.A., for appointment as aide-de-camp on his staff.

By Order Secretary of War
J. C. Bates,
Major General,
Acting Chief of Staff

Douglas was first stunned and then delighted. Joining his father as his aide was the opportunity of a lifetime for Douglas, and within days he was packed and on his way to Japan.

A month before, President Theodore Roosevelt had persuaded the Russians and the Japanese to sign the Treaty of Portsmouth, which ended the Russo-Japanese War. As part of the treaty negotiations, the United States had agreed to recognize Japan's interests in Korea and southern Manchuria, and Japan in turn recognized American interests in the Philippines. Douglas's father was now in Japan trying to work out just what it was that made the Japanese military such an efficient fighting machine.

Douglas arrived in Japan in fine spirits and was immediately off on a tour of Japanese military bases with his father. The two men inspected bases at Nagasaki, Kobe, and Kyoto. Douglas was very impressed with the loyalty and obedience of the Japanese soldiers. His father explained that they would fight to the death for their emperor and country and that the idea of honor meant everything to them. Japanese soldiers routinely committed suicide if they thought they had disgraced themselves or their emperor.

Douglas witnessed the soldiers' obedience firsthand at one of the bases they visited. An epidemic of cholera was sweeping the area, and many of the soldiers at the base were dying from the disease. The Japanese general who commanded the base asked Douglas's advice. "I don't understand it," he said. "Each man has been given a supply of capsules and told to take one every four hours, but the medicine doesn't seem to be working."

Douglas burst out laughing but quickly stopped when he saw the bewildered expression on the general's face. "I'm sorry. I intended no offense," he said. "I was just thinking what American soldiers would do if they were given capsules to take every four hours."

"What would they do?" the Japanese general inquired.

"They would throw the capsules away in the first ditch they came to and forget the whole thing," Douglas said.

"Perhaps that is what they are doing," the general said. "I will fix that."

A few days later the Japanese general came to Douglas with a box. "See, I have had new instructions printed on the capsule boxes," he said. "They say, '*The Emperor requests* that each soldier take one capsule every four hours.'"

Douglas nodded. Within a month the cholera epidemic at the base had ended.

Wherever he went, Douglas took notes on what his father told him and on the conditions he saw around him. After their tour of Japan, the two MacArthurs traveled on to observe military bases in Shanghai, Hong Kong, and the island of Java. They were in Singapore at Christmas and dining with the King of Burma on New Year's Day. Then it was on to Calcutta, the Khyber Pass, and the Chinese cities of Canton, Tsingtao, Peking, Tientsin, and Hankow, and back to Japan in June 1906.

When Douglas tallied it all up, he found that they had traveled twenty thousand miles, inspected hundreds of troops and bases, and talked to every available military leader and government official. Along the way, Douglas had fallen in love with the Orient.

The two MacArthurs spent the first half of July talking with Japanese generals. Douglas wrote in his journal that his father believed that Japan's ambition to expand her borders by taking over nearby countries posed a real threat to peace in the Pacific region. General MacArthur even confided in Douglas that the United States had better build stronger defenses in the Philippines or the Japanese would one day use it as a stepping-stone for their empire building.

On July 17, 1906, Douglas and his father set sail for the United States. As Douglas watched the islands slip over the horizon, he knew that he would find a way one day to return to the Orient.

What Douglas did not know as he made his way back to the United States was that exciting days were just ahead for him. In the fall of 1906 he became a student at the Engineer School at Fort McNair in Washington, D.C. He had just arrived at the school when the director called Douglas into his office and told him that President Theodore Roosevelt had requested that he become an aide-de-camp to the president. Douglas was very surprised at his new post and was eager to learn all he could about politics.

The next two years were divided between duties at the White House and engineer school. Teddy Roosevelt often asked Douglas his opinion on matters pertaining to the Far East, since Douglas had been there and the president had not.

When he graduated from engineer school in 1908, Douglas was ordered to Fort Leavenworth,

Kansas, with the Third Battalion of Engineers. Memories of his childhood there flooded back to him as he walked through the gates of Fort Leavenworth and reported for duty.

As the junior company commander, he was assigned to Company K, the lowest-rated of the twenty-one companies at the post. Douglas threw himself into the job of training the men under his command. He led them on long marches each day to toughen them up physically while he taught them about how to quickly build pontoon bridges on the battlefield and how to be demolition experts. His efforts paid off, and when Company K was again inspected, it was rated the highest of all the companies at the fort.

Douglas continued to impress his superiors and earned the lasting respect of the men under his command over the next four years. Then, on September 5, 1912, Douglas received a telegram that shook his world to the core. The 24th Wisconsin Regiment, the regiment Douglas's father had commanded during the Civil War, was holding its fiftieth reunion in Milwaukee. General MacArthur had been attending the reunion and was making a toast to his old comrades-in-arms when he collapsed and died. Douglas could scarcely take in the news. Yet he knew that it was just the way his father would have wanted to die, in the company of his old army comrades.

The man whose reputation Douglas MacArthur had spent his whole life trying to live up to was now gone. An incredible emptiness swept over Douglas.

Later he wrote, "My whole world changed that night. Never have I been able to heal the wound in my heart." Despite the wound he felt, Douglas determined to throw himself into his military career and become the soldier his father would have been proud of.

Chapter 6

A Mexican Adventure

Soon after his father's funeral, Douglas was transferred to Washington, D.C., where he was made a member of the army and navy's general staff. This division consisted of thirty-eight elite men who worked with the White House to plan the highest-level military operations. Douglas felt this was a tremendous honor, and he worked hard to be as knowledgeable about world situations as he possibly could.

One particular area everyone was keeping a close eye on was Mexico. By 1914 relations between the United States and Mexico had reached a very low point. The year before, Mexican General Victoriano Huerta had overthrown the Mexican government in a bloody uprising, and now he ruled Mexico with a brutal hand.

President Woodrow Wilson grew alarmed as General Huerta tortured and killed American citizens living in Mexico. Douglas and the rest of the general staff in Washington monitored the situation on a daily basis. In early April a group of Mexican soldiers detained a small group of American sailors from several naval vessels sent to protect American interests and citizens in the oil port of Tampico. The Mexican government ordered the immediate release of the sailors and apologized for the incident, but the American government wanted to make the point that this would not be tolerated. It demanded that the American flag be raised in Tampico and that the Mexican garrison stationed in the city fire a twenty-one-gun salute to honor the U.S. flag and all it stood for. This was too much for the Mexican government to agree to.

On April 21, 1914, a fleet of U.S. battleships blockaded the port of Veracruz while a force of American sailors and marines went ashore and occupied the city. An expeditionary force under the command of Major General Funston was dispatched to Veracruz, and preparations to send a larger army were under way. This more permanent army was to be commanded by General Wood.

As part of these preparations, General Wood called Douglas into his office. "I have secret orders for you," he said. "You are to go to Veracruz to assess the situation there for me. If we are to send in a larger army, we need to know exactly what the conditions are on the ground. I am especially interested in what we can expect in the way of transportation to help us push inland."

Douglas immediately set out for Veracruz and arrived in the city on Friday, May 1, 1914. It did not take him long to realize that transportation for a larger American army was going to be a problem. There were virtually no motorized vehicles in the city or surrounding countryside, and few horses or donkeys. There were, however, lots of freight and passenger railcars in the city. The problem was that Douglas could not find any engines to pull them.

The following night Douglas sat in a bar listening to the local patrons talking. He heard one particular drunken man say that he knew where some railway engines were. Douglas took the man aside and plied him with strong coffee. When he had sobered up enough, the man told Douglas that he was a railway engineer and that he had seen a number of engines hidden along the railway line linking Veracruz and the city of Alvarado, farther down the coast.

"I will pay you one hundred fifty dollars in gold if you will lead me to the engines," Douglas told the man.

At first the man was reluctant, explaining that if he were caught leading an American spy into Mexican territory, he would surely be executed. But one hundred fifty dollars was a lot of money, and finally the amount won him over. Despite the danger, the man agreed to lead Douglas, but they would need more help. The man knew two more railroad employees who were also willing to risk their necks for gold.

At dusk two nights later everything was arranged, and Douglas crept across the American frontline undetected and made his way to the rendezvous point just outside Veracruz. Just as planned, the engineer had a handcar waiting for him on the railway line.

Douglas was suspicious of his guide, so before they set out on the handcar, he told the engineer he wanted to search him for weapons. The engineer protested the scrutiny, but Douglas insisted, and finally the man relented. Sure enough, Douglas found a .38-caliber pistol and a knife tucked in the man's belt, and he took both weapons. Then Douglas said to him, "Now it is your turn to search me." The man looked surprised, but Douglas encouraged him to carry out the search. The only thing the man found was Douglas's army-issue revolver, which was in plain sight, holstered to his belt.

"You see," Douglas smiled, "I have nothing of value with me. There would be no point in trying to kill and rob me. When we both return safely, I will give you one hundred fifty dollars." With that understanding the two men set out in the handcar.

Soon they were zipping along the railway line. When they reached the Boca del Rio, they stopped and pulled the handcar off the line and hid it behind some bushes. Because the railroad bridge across the river had collapsed, they crossed the river in a small canoe. On the other side of the river, they met up with the other two men who had been recruited for the operation. These two men had another handcar waiting for them. The four men climbed aboard, and they were once again on their way south.

Douglas was very aware that any Mexican they encountered along the way would know straightaway that he was an American. He needed to keep out of sight, so whenever they approached a small town, they would stop the handcar and Douglas and one of the Mexican men would get off. The other two men would then proceed through the town on the handcar while Douglas and the other man made their way on foot around the town. Douglas made sure that the Mexican man accompanying him was lashed to him so that the man could not run off or become separated in the darkness. On the other side of the town, they would rendezvous with the handcar and set off again on their journey.

Four towns later, Douglas found what he was looking for. It was one o'clock in the morning as they rounded a bend on the handcar, and there before them five railway engines emerged like cold, steel ghosts out of the darkness. The engines were unguarded and parked on a siding. Two of them were switch engines and unsuitable for hauling long, heavy trains, but the other three engines were good for heavy hauling—just what General Wood needed to advance American troops deeper into Mexico.

After Douglas had inspected the engines, it was time to head back to Veracruz. As he retraced his path around the small town of Salinas, Douglas came face-to-face with five armed bandits. He and his Mexican companion made a run for it in the darkness, and the men opened fire on them and gave chase. The two of them ran as fast as they could. Douglas could feel his heart pounding as he pushed himself on at a full sprint. Finally three of the bandits gave up the chase, but two of them kept coming and soon gained on Douglas and his companion. There was only one thing to do. Douglas reached for his revolver, swung around, and opened fire, killing both men.

After the ordeal they rejoined the other two men on the handcar and sped along the tracks as fast as their arms could pump the lever.

By the time they reached the next town, Piedra, a thick mist had settled over the area. Once again Douglas and a companion set off to detour around the outskirts of the town on foot. In the mist they managed to walk right into the middle of another group of armed bandits, this time fifteen of them on horseback. The bandits opened fire in the mist, and one of their bullets grazed Douglas's companion's shoulder, while three bullets grazed past Douglas so close that they tore holes in his jacket. Once again Douglas was forced to pull out his revolver and open fire. He was not sure how many of the bandits he hit, but he saw at least four men topple from their horses. In the mayhem that followed, Douglas grabbed his companion and escaped into the darkness.

Once again they rendezvoused with the handcar and sped off. Douglas hoped desperately that they had seen their last bandits for the night, but yet another band awaited them as they approached Laguna.

Bullets whizzed through the air again as three mounted bandits fired on the handcar. Douglas, the only one of the four with a gun, steadied his hand and took aim as the riders came closer. One bullet found its mark. The lead horse reared up and fell sideways, nearly knocking the handcar off the tracks, while the bandit on the animal's back crashed to the ground. The other two bandits quickly fled.

Finally Douglas and his three companions reached the Boca del Rio, where they left the handcar and quickly made their way back across the river. On the way the canoe was punctured by a submerged branch and sank, forcing the men to wade the rest of the way in chest-deep water. Douglas wondered whether this deadly night would ever end.

On the other side of the Boca del Rio, the men quickly located the other handcar and lifted it onto the railway line. Soon they were speeding along the line toward Veracruz. There were no more bandits, and the four men secretly crossed the American front line just before dawn and made their way back into the city, exhausted and glad to be alive.

As the sun rose across Campeche Bay, Douglas led the men back to his room and gave them each one hundred fifty dollars worth of gold. He was sorry to see them go. They had begun the night deeply suspicious of each other, but a bond had developed between them as they had accomplished their dangerous mission together.

After he had rested, Douglas wrote a report on what he had seen along the way and the state of the engines he had discovered, and he quickly dispatched the report to General Wood in Washington.

In July 1914, however, General Huerta fled Mexico, and the standoff with the Mexican government waned. As a result it was decided that a large American army would not be sent to Veracruz, and the railway engines Douglas had riskéd his life to locate and survey would not be needed to transport troops inland after all.

Douglas was ordered to return to his desk job in Washington. A major war had erupted in Europe because of strong nationalist movements as well as imperialistic, territorial, and economic rivalries between the great Western powers. The United States was keeping a close eye on events there. As the war dragged on, a rift developed between President Woodrow Wilson and Douglas's boss, Secretary of War Lindley Garrison. The two men disagreed about whether American troops should join in the war on the side of Britain and France and their allies against the alliance known as the Central Powers—Germany, Austria-Hungary, and the Ottoman Empire. President Wilson was against it; he wanted to see the Europeans negotiate a peace treaty. Finally the rift came to a head in February 1916 with the resignation of Secretary Garrison and his assistant. A new man, Newton Baker, was quickly appointed in Garrison's place. One of the first things Secretary Baker did after taking up his new assignment was to name Douglas MacArthur as the head of the Bureau of Information for the War Department. The job involved explaining the national military policy to the press and through them to the American people. Douglas's aim was to prepare the American population for the time when the United States might become involved in the war in Europe.

On April 6, 1917, President Wilson could no longer ignore the number of American ships that German submarines had sunk in the Atlantic Ocean, and so the United States declared war on Germany.

Immediately Douglas was bombarded with the question of which army divisions would be sent to France first to join the Allies in the fight against the Central Powers. It seemed to him that the entire nation was waiting to find out. Some states felt that their divisions should have the honor of being the first to go to France, while other states made it clear that they did not want their fighting men to be the first to die on foreign soil.

Secretary Baker called Douglas into his office to discuss the matter.

"You know how difficult this whole business is," Baker began. "I have no idea how to solve the issue in a fair manner. The last thing we need to do here is inflame the American people."

Douglas thought for a moment, and suddenly an idea struck him. "What if we take National Guard units from many different states and form a division that would stretch over the country like a rainbow?" he suggested.

"That's it!" Baker exclaimed. "A rainbow division. No one can argue with that! That's its name, the Rainbow Division. And I know just the man to command it—Brigadier General Mann."

"I agree," Douglas said, "but we must remember that the brigadier general is approaching retirement age and his health is poor. He'll need the best colonel available to be his chief of staff."

Secretary Baker nodded. "I have already made my selection for that post." Then he stood up and slapped Douglas's shoulder. "It is you!"

For once in his life Douglas MacArthur was too flabbergasted to speak. "But...but...I mean I am honored, but I'm not a colonel," he finally stammered.

"You are now," Baker said. "I will sign your commission immediately. I take it you want to stay in the Corps of Engineers?"

In that second Douglas thought of his father in the 24th Wisconsin infantry. "No, sir," he told the secretary. "I believe I want to transfer to the infantry."

"Very well. It shall be done," Baker said. "Prepare to go to France!"

Chapter 7

On the Western Front

Douglas strolled around the wooden shacks that housed the twenty-seven thousand men of the Rainbow Division. Just as he had suggested, they had been drawn from all forty-eight states, and now they were assembled at Camp Mills, near Garden City on Long Island, training around the clock until they were a tight fighting unit.

By October, three months after Douglas had won his new appointment of colonel, the Rainbow Division was ready to set sail for France. It boarded a convoy of newly outfitted army transport ships, and Douglas was pleased to learn that his brother Arthur was commanding the *Chattanooga*, one of the naval ships escorting the convoy across the Atlantic Ocean. The voyage was supposed to take fourteen days, but everyone, including Douglas, was aware that one in four American ships that began the journey across the Atlantic was sunk at sea by the Germans.

From their first day out of port, the men aboard the ships in the convoy followed very strict orders. To avoid attracting the attention of German U-boats, they were not allowed to smoke in the open, and all lights had to be turned off at night. Everyone wore his life preserver at all times, and the lifeboats were lowered to deck level for a fast escape.

The crews of the various ships in the convoy were constantly engaged in target practice, aiming their vessels' guns at targets towed behind the ships. One nervous day followed another, until ten of the fourteen days had passed.

Four days out from their destination of St. Nazaire, France, the captain of the transport ship *Covington,* on which Douglas was sailing, informed Douglas that they were headed into a very active zone known for submarine attacks and mines. For the next three days the captain never left the bridge. His life, and the life of every man aboard the ship, depended on his sighting the enemy and taking swift evasive action.

Twenty-four hours off the French coast, the ship's horns blared, summoning all aboard to battle stations. Enemy submarines had been spotted. The captain ordered evasive maneuvers, changing the course of the ship by forty-five degrees. Through the darkness Douglas could hear the distant warning sirens of the other ships in the convoy. He hoped and prayed that all of the ships and all of his men would make it safely to France.

When the sun arose the next morning, Douglas was amazed and grateful to learn that the entire convoy had survived. It was a rare event, one all of his men celebrated with him. That evening they spotted the lights of Belle Isle, and soon the *Covington* was steaming into the harbor at St. Nazaire, located at the mouth of the Loire River. They had completed the first stage of their mission. Now it was time to fight the Germans.

Since 1914 the war in France had been fought in the trenches. France was divided by two parallel lines of trenches, which ran all the way from the English Channel to the Swiss border, a total of 466 miles. The German troops were on the eastern side of the trenches, and the French and English were on the western side. For three years both sides had sat in almost stationary positions, taking potshots at each other and occasionally running raids into the other's territory. Sometimes one side gained a few yards and dug a new trench; other times they lost ground. Each skirmish was bloody. In one battle the French gained seven hundred yards of land but lost twenty-six thousand men in doing so.

Once it arrived in France, the Rainbow Division made its way to Rolampont in the Meuse River Valley near the western front, where the men set up headquarters. It was early November, and many of the men were billeted with local French farmers and villagers. It was a bitter-cold winter, the coldest in fifty years, but Douglas insisted on drilling his men so that they would be ready for battle in the spring.

As it turned out, it was Douglas who had the first opportunity to engage the enemy. He thought it was important to see their new enemy up close before leading his men into battle against them. So when Douglas learned that a group of French soldiers were planning a raid behind German lines, he asked French General de Bazelair if he could accompany the raiding party. The general was reluctant to expose an American officer to such danger, but Douglas pressed him until he agreed. The raid was set for the night of February 26, 1918.

When Douglas arrived at the French line, the soldiers looked surprised to see him and the clothes he was wearing. Douglas wore a smashed-down cap instead of a steel helmet and had a four-foot-long muffler his mother had knit wrapped around his neck. Douglas completed his outfit with a turtleneck sweater, perfectly pressed riding pants, and cavalry boots polished until they almost glowed in the encroaching darkness. His only weapon was a riding crop.

Douglas joined the French soldiers as they daubed black mud on their faces and then crawled into the frontline trench. Everyone waited nervously for the order to go over the top. In the silence a French lieutenant handed Douglas a pair of wire cutters and a trench knife. Douglas slid the wire cutters into the pocket of his pants and the knife into his belt.

Finally the order was given. Douglas watched as the first wave of French soldiers climbed up over the edge of the trench and began crawling on their bellies across the no-man's-land between the French and German lines. He followed and soon found himself slithering through oozing mud that was littered with shell casings and smashed and splintered pieces of wood that Douglas supposed had once been trees. Soon they found themselves crawling over mangled bodies, all that was left of both French and German soldiers who had attempted missions like this before.

As the raiding party cut its way through the snarl of barbed wire that blocked its way, flares suddenly lit up the sky. The Germans had spotted them! Almost at once came the rattle of machine-gun fire, and shards of hot lead rained down on the French raiders. Douglas watched in horror as several soldiers around him were hit and killed. He quickly redoubled his effort to hack through the barbed wire with his wire cutters. Despite the ferocious gunfire, the French soldiers kept advancing until they reached the edge of the German trench. Douglas slid the trench knife from his belt and leapt into the trench with the rest of the French raiders. Finally he was looking directly into the eyes of the enemy.

As more and more French raiders piled into the German trench, the machine guns eventually fell silent, and brutal hand-to-hand combat began. As soldiers fell dead around him, Douglas fought for his life. It seemed forever until the French soldiers got the upper hand and the Germans fled into the night. By then Douglas had a German colonel pinned down, and he decided to take him prisoner rather than slit his throat. When Douglas arrived back in the trench with his German prisoner, the French soldiers applauded him for his bravery during the raid, and General de Bazelair pinned a

Croix de Guerre on him to recognize and reward his gallantry.

A week later the Rainbow Division prepared for action. The division was ordered to attack a section of the German trenches on the Salient du Feys on the night of March 9, and Douglas intended to accompany the men into battle.

As the hour approached when the American soldiers were scheduled to storm the German line, the German artillery opened fire on the American line. Somehow, Douglas concluded, they had been tipped off. Before they had even left their trenches, American soldiers were riddled with holes, victims of German shrapnel. Douglas was soon marching up and down the American line, encouraging the men to hold the line and keep up their courage.

Finally, five minutes before zero hour, sixty French artillery batteries returned fire on the Germans. As the French shells found their mark, the German artillery fire subsided.

At the appointed hour Douglas gave the order for his men to advance. The men scurried up ladders and over the edge of the trench and made their way toward the German line. A seemingly endless swell of American soldiers with gleaming bayonets swept into the German trenches, quickly overrunning the enemy.

For their efforts in the battle, the men of the Rainbow Division won the admiration of both the British and the French troops they fought alongside, and Douglas was awarded a Distinguished Service Cross.

Soon afterward the Germans mounted a counteroffensive, and for eighty-two days the Rainbow Division was involved in almost constant combat as it fought to hold its line and beat back the enemy. Finally, on June 21, the Americans were relieved from the fighting for some well-earned rest.

More battles followed for the Rainbow Division. The men fought courageously despite sometimes experiencing heavy casualties. As new recruits arrived to replace those who had been killed or wounded in the fighting, Douglas made sure they were trained and made ready for battle. He was dismayed on one occasion to learn that a group of new recruits had just arrived from the United States without any training in how to shoot and maintain a rifle. Douglas ordered his officers to work with the men around the clock until they could fire their rifles straight and hit a target.

Throughout the fighting Douglas continued to show courage on the field of battle, earning many medals for his bravery and inspiring the officers and men serving under him. Douglas was soon promoted to the rank of brigadier general in command of the Rainbow Division. His childhood friend Billy Hughes took his former position as chief of staff.

Unlike most of the other American and Allied generals in France, Douglas was not comfortable stuck in a command post well behind his troops, giving orders and poring over maps to learn how the war was going. Instead he wanted to be right on the front line with his troops, encouraging them and seeing the progress of the battle firsthand so that he could issue orders to respond to new situations as they arose.

In July 1918 the German army launched an all-out offensive to break through the Allied lines and once and for all win the war. However, things did not go as planned for the Germans. French and American forces, including the Rainbow Division, managed to crush the western flank of the German line at Chateau Thierry. From there they relentlessly pursued the retreating Germans. Within a month the Allies had taken one hundred thousand German soldiers prisoner. Still, the Germans refused to give up the fight and made a determined stand at a group of hills known as the Côte-de-Châtillon. Several American divisions had been decimated trying to wrestle the Côte-de-Châtillon from the Germans. From its high ground, the German army was able to rake the advancing American forces with gunfire and stop their advance.

The Rainbow Division was moved in to assist its fellow American divisions. When he arrived at the battleground, Douglas quickly familiarized himself with the countryside. Rolling hills and wooded valleys stretched before them, with the Germans firmly in control of the high, rocky ridges. Douglas understood why the American forces were having so much difficulty taking the position. They were attacking the center of the German line, where they had to negotiate through a tangle of barbed wire stretched out by the Germans. As the Americans tried to make their way through this tangle, German gunners, from their high vantage points, mowed them down.

Douglas observed that on the far left and right flanks of the German position the barbed wire petered out. This was the Germans' weak point, and Douglas intended to exploit it. It would not be an easy fight: the terrain was treacherous, with little cover in some places. Douglas quickly divided the Rainbow Division in two, with one half attacking the Germans' left flank and the other half their right flank, while artillery rained down on the center of the German line.

On the cold, misty morning of October 12 the battle began. Allied artillery fire slammed into the German line as the men of the Rainbow Division moved out. The fighting was fierce, and the casualties quickly mounted, but the Americans kept advancing. Douglas ordered his men to break into small groups and creep forward on their bellies, using every shattered stump and rock they could find for cover from the German gunfire. By the end of the day, the Americans had captured Hill 288, one of the hills that made up the Côte-de-Châtillon.

That night Douglas readjusted his plans and sent out runners with new orders for his men. The following day the men of the Rainbow Division fought their way up the nine-hundred-foot-high Hill 282 and captured it from the enemy. Then they captured the Tuilieres Ferme. From there they closed in on the final fortifications of the Côte-de-Châtillon. From the left and the right the American forces moved in a pincer movement, eventually overrunning the German position. The Côte-de-Châtillon had finally been captured and the German guns silenced.

It was a brilliant victory, but the victory had come at a high price. Out of 1,450 men and 25 officers who made up one of the companies of the Rainbow Division, only 300 men and 6 officers had survived the fighting. The other companies that made up the division reported similar losses. Still, the victory allowed the American forces to continue their advance.

The American forces were still advancing against the German positions when, on November 11, 1918, a treaty ended the fighting. The Germans had been beaten. The war was over.

On April 25, 1919, exactly eighteen months after they had set out for France, Douglas MacArthur, the most decorated American soldier of the war, and his troops arrived home in the United States. As they marched down the gangplank of the *Leviathan* and onto the dock, it was a bittersweet moment. Behind Douglas marched the bravest group of men he had ever known. They had spent 224 days facing the Germans on the western front in France, with 162 of those days being spent in combat. In the course of the fighting, 2,713 men had been killed and 14,683 wounded. In front of Douglas and the men of the Rainbow Division lay the great city of New York, yet not a single person turned out to welcome them home. Only a street urchin stopped to wave as they marched off the *Leviathan*.

To Douglas it was a sad and gloomy end to a great division, and it left him wondering whether he had a future in the army.

Chapter 8

Promotion

The Great War in Europe became known as the War to End All Wars, and Douglas MacArthur soon found that most Americans embraced the slogan. They believed that the Allies had made such an example of the German kaiser and his troops that no ruler or country in Europe, or anywhere else for that matter, would dare to strike out against peaceful countries again, involving them in a bloody world war. Douglas, on the other hand, held the opposite view. He became alarmed when he learned the terms of the armistice that the Allies had forced Germany to sign. The terms seemed to him too harsh, and in a letter to one of his former aides he wrote, "We are wondering here what is to happen with reference to the peace terms. They look drastic and seem to me more like a treaty of perpetual war than that of perpetual peace."

Unlike most Americans, Douglas had a special interest in predicting whether the United States would go to war again. Upon his return he had been appointed to a position he had never imagined holding—superintendent of West Point. But the job did not hold the honor it had once held. Because of the war, the normal four-year course had been shortened to a single year, and much of the protocol and ceremony that had been a part of the experience of attending the military academy was gone. To make matters worse, the expectation that all war might now be over was leading Congress to question the need for West Point. What was the point of training army officers if there was to be no more war? And couldn't the country better use the money it spent on West Point for other things?

Once Douglas understood how desperate the situation was, he went straight to Washington to lobby for his institution. He argued that over nine thousand West Point graduates had been killed in the Great War and they needed to be replaced with officers of equal training as soon as possible. Any country that did not pay attention to its ongoing defense because of some fuzzy notion about there never again being another war was placing itself in peril. In August Douglas returned from Washington with a promise that West Point would go on.

In the meantime, while he was in Washington, Douglas had invited his aging mother to live with him at West Point, which she was glad to do. During the war she had lived with his brother Arthur's wife and children.

With the matter of West Point's future settled, Douglas began assessing the internal problems of the academy. And there were many. The institution had to be reestablished as a four-year program. But since there were no upperclassmen, the plebes would have to be the senior classmen for the next three years. And many of the courses taught at the academy were not up-to-date with the new post–world war era. For example, while he was in France, Douglas had been impressed with the potential of using airplanes in war, but West Point had no courses on how to use them for reconnaissance to gather information for the troops fighting on the ground. Nor did it have courses that taught officers how to deal with the kinds of trench warfare they had encountered there.

Modernizing West Point was not an easy task, especially since many of the instructors had been at the institution when Douglas was a cadet, and they considered him far too young for the position. Despite the opposition, Douglas managed to make many positive changes at West Point. He allowed the cadets more freedom, giving them weekend passes and a five-dollar-a-month allowance. He banned hazing and did away with the Beast Barracks. Instead he sent cadets off to regular army training posts to learn about and practice modern warfare. Douglas also made participation in team sports compulsory, and he even composed a verse as to why this was necessary. He had it carved above the portals to the gymnasium:

Upon the fields of friendly strife
Are sown the seeds
That, upon other fields, on other days
Will bear the fruits of victory.

The Rainbow Division in which Douglas had been promoted to the rank of brigadier general had been made up of National Guard troops from the various states. But in January 1920 Douglas was appointed a brigadier general in the regular army. As he accepted the promotion, Douglas wished his father could have been there to see him receive the honor.

Two years later Douglas was as astonished as everyone else to find that he had asked a woman to marry him! Louise Cromwell Brooks was ten years younger than Douglas and a world apart in just about every other way. As the stepdaughter of Edward Stotesbury, who, with a fortune of over one hundred million dollars, was one of the richest men in America, Louise had grown up in the midst of extreme wealth. Although she had been exposed to a broad cultural education, a disciplined character had not been one of its benefits. Before meeting Douglas, Louise had been married and had two children, but during the war years her marriage had collapsed, and she was now a single mother. Douglas had met Louise at a resort about twenty miles from West Point and was immediately smitten with her. They talked until midnight, and then Douglas asked her to marry him. She agreed, and they set January 15, 1922, as the date for the wedding.

News of the engagement was soon making headlines in the newspapers. And then, shortly afterward, Douglas was once again in the headlines. This time the headlines announced that his tenure at West Point was to end early and that he was to be posted to the Philippines as the new commander of the Military District of Manila.

Following a lavish marriage ceremony at Louise's stepfather's house in Palm Beach, Florida, and a short honeymoon, preparations got under way to be in the Philippines before the end of the year.

In October 1922 Douglas, Louise, and her two young children, Walter Jr. and little Louise, peered out over Manila Bay from the bow of the *Thomas.* Their ten-thousand-mile voyage from the United States was over. It had been eighteen years since Douglas was last in the Far East, and he looked forward to getting back into active army life. He hoped that Louise was just as excited as he was, though something told him that the young socialite at his side would have a difficult time adjusting to this new life.

Many things had changed in the Philippines since Douglas was last there. The Filipinos were demanding they be given more say over their country, and Douglas agreed with them. He saw these demands as part of the process toward independence, and he gladly welcomed Manuel Quezon and other Philippine officials into his home. This caused a rift with some of the older army officers, who had lost contact with the local people and considered themselves colonial rulers.

One year after arriving in the Philippines, Douglas received some crushing news. His only surviving brother, Arthur, had died of appendicitis. It was an unexpected blow, and Louise was not very sympathetic. So Christmas 1923 turned out to be a rather grim affair for the MacArthur family. Douglas was in mourning over the death of his brother, little Louise had a severe bout of malaria, and Walter Jr. had fallen off his horse and broken several bones. Meanwhile Louise, who was more of a socialite than a general's wife, was complaining about how bored she was and how she would rather be almost anywhere else in the entire world.

Still, Douglas tried not to let these things get him down. He kept busy in Manila. He surveyed and mapped areas on the Bataan peninsula across Manila Bay, and he oversaw the building of new bridges and roads. His ultimate aim was to see the Philippines become completely independent. However, a promotion made him overqualified for the post he held in the Philippines. On January 17, 1925, Douglas was awarded his second star and promoted in rank to major general. At forty-five years of age, he was the youngest major general in the United States army.

Louise could not contain her delight when Douglas announced that he had been transferred back to the United States. Douglas's next post was command of the Third Corps, headquartered in Baltimore, Maryland, just a few miles from where Louise owned a luxurious estate. The MacArthur family moved into the estate, which was renamed

Rainbow Hill, and Douglas drove an automobile to work each day from the estate to the headquarters of the Third Corps.

Now that they were back in the United States, Louise took a firm hand in the couple's social life. She organized a never-ending round of foxhunts, dinner parties, and golf tournaments for Douglas to participate in. She also invited her stepfather and brother to visit. Wall Street was booming at the time, and since both men were making a fortune on the stock market, they tried hard to persuade Douglas to leave the army and become a stockbroker.

Douglas soon tired of all the social activity, and Louise was busy making a life of her own. More and more it was being rumored that the company she was keeping would not be good for her family life.

In 1927 the director of the American Olympic team died unexpectedly. In the rush for a new director to be appointed, Douglas's name came up as a candidate. Douglas gratefully accepted the challenge, and after being given detached service from the army, he threw his heart and soul into whipping the team into shape in time for the Amsterdam Olympics the following year.

It was a wonderful nine months for Douglas, who loved sports and loved pushing his team to do the very best they could. He trained the athletes as if they were recruits at boot camp.

When they arrived in Amsterdam to participate in the Olympic Games, Douglas gave the American team a pep talk. "Americans never quit," he began.

"We are here to represent the greatest country on earth. We did not come here to lose gracefully. We came here to win—and win decisively." And win they did. The American team won twenty-two gold medals, eighteen silver medals, and sixteen bronze medals, more than twice as many medals as any other country.

When he returned to the United States after the Olympic Games in Amsterdam, Douglas received the unexpected news that he had been ordered to return to Manila for two years to assume command of all American forces in the Philippines.

The new assignment made Douglas very happy, but his marital situation did not. Instead of returning to the Philippines with her husband, Louise decided that she and the children would stay behind in the United States. Although it was not publicly announced, Douglas understood that when he left for the Philippines, she was going to file for divorce from him. It was a situation he could do little about.

Chapter 9

Army Chief of Staff

Douglas had been in the Philippines only a few weeks when the divorce from Louise became final. It was a difficult time for him personally, but he threw himself into his work.

As could be expected, things had changed in the Philippines during his absence. One alarming change was the number of Japanese workers flooding into the southern Philippine island of Mindanao. Douglas thought many of them were probably spies, and he was very concerned about how the Philippines would defend itself if the Japanese chose to invade the country. At the same time, the United States Congress was busy cutting money from the military budget.

Things became even more desperate when the American economy nose-dived into a severe depression after the Wall Street crash of 1929. Because of the constant shortage of money, his two-year tour of duty in the Philippines proved to be a very difficult time for Douglas, who grew weary of constantly having to point out the need for more equipment and trained men and receiving little of what he asked for.

At the end of his two-year posting in the Philippines, Douglas received a remarkable appointment. On August 6, 1930, President Hoover announced that Douglas would be the next army chief of staff, the highest-ranking officer in the army. The president said that he had "searched the army for younger blood" and "finally determined upon General Douglas MacArthur. His brilliant abilities and sterling character need no exposition from me."

Douglas lost no time in setting sail for home, and on November 21, 1930, he was sworn in to his new position. At fifty years of age, he was the youngest chief of staff in American history. He moved into the quarters that came with the position, Fort Myer Number One, a luxurious brick home set on the west bank of the Potomac River. His mother, who had been living with Arthur's widow, moved in with him once again.

As the months went by, Douglas had to admit that, although he did not expect things to go smoothly, he faced more challenges in the new job than he had imagined. The economy had slumped into a terrible state, and every government department had to make huge budget cuts. Everywhere men were out of work, families were being evicted from their homes or were simply walking off their farms, and young people were forced to leave school or college early to try to support their families.

Back in 1924 Congress had passed an act mandating that the veterans of the Great War were due to be paid a bonus in 1945. However, as the Great Depression tightened its grip on the American population, Congressman Wright Pullman introduced a bill in the House of Representatives that would authorize the government to pay the bonuses immediately instead of waiting that long. He argued that the veterans needed the money to eat and that many of them might starve before they ever collected a penny. By May 1932 thousands of veterans, many of them hungry and penniless, had descended on Washington to encourage the immediate passage of Congressman Pullman's bill. The veterans camped out in shacks and tents on the edge of Washington and held daily marches to Capitol Hill and the White House. Newspapers dubbed the protest the Bonus March. And as the Bonus March grew in strength, President Hoover and many politicians, as well as Douglas, worried that it might get out of hand.

Douglas knew that many of those involved in the Bonus March were veterans, but he was convinced that Communist organizers had infiltrated the veterans' ranks and were using the march to stir up trouble in the hope that they could eventually overthrow the government. Douglas kept a careful eye on the situation, and he became even more concerned as he saw that the D.C. police force was having a difficult time controlling the crowd.

Eventually the House of Representatives passed the bill authorizing the payment of the bonus, but the Senate did not, and President Hoover declared that he would veto the bill if the Senate did pass it. Faced with this outcome, many of the veterans lost heart and left the capital, but about ten thousand stayed on to protest.

The situation grew more tense with each passing day, until on July 28, 1932, things boiled over. During a demonstration the D.C. police opened fire on the demonstrators, killing several of them. Fearing that the situation was about to get completely out of hand, the police chief appealed to President Hoover for help. Minutes after the request was made, Douglas received written orders from the White House to use army troops to clear the streets of Washington.

Douglas sprang into action at once. Six hundred soldiers from nearby army bases were ordered to assemble at the Washington Monument, where Douglas joined them and took command of the operation. The soldiers were ordered not to fire on the crowd. Instead they closed in on the demonstrators, who were now gathered at the foot of Capitol Hill, and used tear gas to disperse them. Once that was accomplished, Douglas ordered his men to move out to the edge of the city and destroy the shantytown the protesters had erected there. His mission complete, Douglas then went to the White House and reported to the president.

In the aftermath of the breaking up of the Bonus March, Douglas was criticized by many. They thought it was despicable to order that tear gas be used against hungry protesters, many of whom had fought under him in France. The criticism stung

Douglas, who explained that it tasted like gall to him—a taste that would stay with him for a long time. But he believed he had done the right thing. Not only had he followed orders, but also in doing so he believed that he had cut short a Communist revolt against the government.

In January 1933 Franklin D. Roosevelt was sworn in as the thirty-second president of the United States. He brought with him to Washington the promises of a "new deal"—welfare relief and more jobs for the poorest Americans. But the money to fund these promises had to come from somewhere, and Douglas was appalled when the new president ordered him to slash the army budget by 51 percent. In a storm of protest Douglas threatened to resign, but President Roosevelt told him not to be foolish. He explained that given the economic state the nation was in, the entire country, including the army, was going to have to make sacrifices.

In the end Douglas stayed on as President Roosevelt's army chief of staff, but it was an uneasy partnership. Douglas watched powerlessly as Japanese aggression and expansion grew in the Far East and as Adolf Hitler built up the German army.

Whenever he could, Douglas encouraged the American people to think about defending themselves in the next war. But he was criticized as being an officer on the lookout for a fight. In response to this criticism Douglas wrote:

We keep the peace; we don't make wars. We are not called in until after the statesmen have decided to fight it out. No military man has ever made or recommended war, as our historic records show. No man abhors war more than that Regular Army man, no man more than I do. There is no glory in war—no shining armor or even bright uniforms. The battlefield is a place of blood and stench and filth.

But nobody—statesmen or governments—has discovered a way to eliminate war. They talk about it every so often, but they never get anywhere, as witness the League of Nations and the disarmament conferences. There is no alchemy by which men can be prevented from settling their difficulties by force. Nothing has changed so little as human nature. And until governments refuse to use force in their intercourse, it is common sense and decency to be prepared. It is only fair to give a fifty-fifty chance to the soldiers.

Meanwhile Douglas kept an ear open for any changes in policy toward the Philippines. He finally learned that the United States government was interested in making the Philippines, now a U.S. commonwealth, into an independent nation sooner rather than later. As a result it had set a goal for complete independence by July 4, 1946. If this timetable was followed, it would mean that the United States had been "helping" the Philippines toward independence for forty-eight years, after liberating the islands from Spain in the Spanish-American War.

Douglas's tenure as army chief of staff ended in the summer of 1935, and Douglas was left with a dilemma. What should he do next? He had nine years left until retirement, and he had already held the top army post in the nation.

The answer to his dilemma came from his old friend in the Philippines, Manuel Quezon. By now Quezon was the leading politician in the Philippines and was sure to be elected the first president of the emerging commonwealth. Because of Japanese expansion in the region, Manuel Quezon needed someone to help build up the Philippine defenses and develop a strong military. He offered the job to Douglas, who was quick to take it up.

The whole plan worked out wonderfully. President Roosevelt allowed Douglas to remain on active duty in the army while he served as a military adviser to the Philippine government.

By the end of November, everything was settled, and Douglas set out for Manila yet again. This time traveling with Douglas were his eighty-three-year-old mother; his sister-in-law Mary, who was acting as his mother's nurse; an army doctor; Major Dwight Eisenhower, his new chief of staff in the Philippines; and his four aides. The voyage across the Pacific Ocean was relatively quiet, and Douglas spent a lot of time with his mother. Although he was reluctant to believe it at first, it was becoming increasingly obvious that Pinky MacArthur was slowly slipping away.

While on board the ship, Douglas did manage to attend a few dinner parties, and at one of them he met a thirty-seven-year-old woman named Jean

Faircloth Douglas. Everyone traveling with him liked her at once. Although Jean was only five feet tall, she was a bundle of energy and enthusiasm. And when she realized that Pinky MacArthur was so ill, she did all she could to help ease the family's burden.

In fact, Douglas soon discovered that Jean Faircloth Douglas and his mother had a lot in common. The two women were from staunch southern stock. And as they talked, Douglas learned that Jean's grandfather had been a captain in the Confederate army and had fought against his father at the Battle of Missionary Ridge. Jean's father had become a wealthy flour mill owner and had left her enough money to spend the rest of her life traveling around the world.

Jean's next stop was supposed to be Shanghai, but after meeting Douglas, she changed her plans and offered to stay with the MacArthur family to help nurse Pinky.

Douglas was grateful for Jean's help, as he had a lot of work to accomplish once he arrived in the Philippines. On the ship during the voyage over, Douglas and his assistants had devised a plan that needed to be put into practice as soon as possible. The plan called for an army made up of a group of permanent soldiers, who in turn would train forty thousand Filipino citizen-soldiers each year at one hundred camps spread throughout the Philippine Islands. Douglas calculated that in ten years, when the country was completely independent, four hundred thousand well-trained soldiers would be ready for service when needed. He also set about planning for an air force with 250 planes and a navy made up of 50 PT boats armed with torpedoes. Manuel Quezon had already committed the Philippines to pay the eight million dollars the plan would cost, and President Roosevelt agreed that the United States government would either provide the equipment on loan or sell it to the Philippine government at cost.

Two months after her arrival in Manila, Pinky MacArthur died of a blood clot in her brain. Douglas arranged to have her temporarily buried in a local cemetery, though as soon as it was practical, he planned to have her body exhumed and buried next to his father at Arlington National Cemetery in Virginia. Although Douglas had been expecting it, he still found his mother's death a heavy blow to bear. Now all of the people in his immediate family were dead, and he felt very alone.

Still, despite his feelings of loneliness, he had a job to do, and he was determined to do it right.

Chapter 10

Corregidor

Douglas immediately set about preparing a national Filipino army. This was not an easy task, particularly when the money and supplies promised from America did not arrive. Political wrangling back in the United States had delayed most of the help, except for a few British Enfield rifles left over from the Great War.

It was a great relief when Manuel Quezon invited Douglas to accompany him on a tour of Japan, the United States, and Mexico. Douglas hoped that as a result of the tour he would be able to bring back more money and supplies. Regrettably, this did not happen. The two men were virtually ignored by both the United States Congress and President Roosevelt, who felt that they had more pressing things to worry about, particularly the buildup of Adolf Hitler's army in Germany.

One good thing did come out of the trip, however. While in the United States, Douglas married Jean Faircloth Douglas at the Municipal Building in New York City on April 30, 1937. His second wedding was as different from his first as anyone could imagine. There was no media hoopla, no important guests, just Jean, Douglas, and two of his officers who acted as witnesses. That was the way Douglas wanted it, and Jean was happy to go along with his wishes. Following the wedding the couple enjoyed a quiet honeymoon, and then it was time to head back to the Philippines.

Ten months after their wedding, on February 21, 1938, Jean gave birth to a son, whom they named Arthur. Although Douglas was fifty-eight years old, he was excited to be a father and doted on his new son.

The world Arthur was born into was not a peaceful one. By the time he was two years old, war was once again erupting around the world. Japan had invaded China, and the German military was on the move. First the Germans overran Poland with alarming ease, and then they turned their attention to France and Great Britain.

The Japanese aggression in China had finally opened Congress's eyes to Japan's intentions in the region. Congress realized that because of its strategic position, the Japanese saw the Philippines as a stepping-off point to controlling the entire Pacific region. As a result Douglas was appointed commander in chief of all American troops in the Far East, and Congress did what it could to help him build up the strength of the Philippine army, air force, and navy.

On August 15, 1941, Congress went further and inducted members of the Philippine air force and infantry into the service of the United States. Even so, the buildup of troops and equipment in the Philippines was going much too slowly for Douglas. By December ground forces consisted of fewer than 12,000 American troops, the same number of Filipino scouts, and 110,000 soldiers in the Citizen National Army. The navy had three cruisers, thirteen destroyers, eighteen submarines, and six PT boats. The Japanese, on the other hand, had six million soldiers at their disposal, and Douglas was sure that they would invade the country soon. He worked frantically to ready the troops for such an invasion.

On the morning of December 8, 1941, Douglas was awakened from a deep sleep by the ringing of a telephone. He glanced at the time—3:40 AM. Bleary eyed, he reached over and picked up the receiver.

"General, this is Sutherland here. Sorry to disturb you, sir," came the voice of his chief of staff. "I knew you would want to know, sir. The Japanese have just bombed Pearl Harbor."

"Pearl Harbor!" Douglas exploded, wide awake in an instant. "That should be our strongest point. Meet me in my office."

Douglas put down the telephone and tried to take in what he had just heard. In the past couple of weeks, squadrons of Japanese aircraft had been flying over the Philippines, and Douglas expected some kind of strike against American interests in Asia. But Pearl Harbor! Pearl Harbor was in Hawaii, an American territory geographically closer to the United States than it was to Asia. Douglas was dumbfounded.

As Douglas buttoned his shirt, the phone rang again. This time it was the War Department in Washington, D.C., confirming the attack and adding that the Japanese had done considerable damage to the American Pacific fleet at anchor in the harbor.

Ten minutes later Douglas was in his office, with his chief of staff and aides milling around him. Like Douglas they were barely able to take in the audaciousness of the Japanese attack. They wondered aloud about what would happen next. For once Douglas MacArthur was too shocked to know what might come next. He refused to believe that the Japanese would attack the Philippines so quickly after its attack on Pearl Harbor. But he was wrong. Just after noon that day a squadron of two hundred Japanese airplanes swooped down on Clark Air Force Base, forty miles to the north of Manila. They hit the men and planes on the ground at the air force base in three waves. First came their heavy bombers. These were followed by dive-bombers, and finally fighters raked the ground with machine-gun fire.

Before the phone rang telling him of the attack, Douglas had already spotted from his penthouse apartment at the Manila Hotel a column of black smoke rising from the direction of Clark Air Force

Base. He could hardly bear to think of the destruction it represented.

When the numbers were tallied, the United States forces in the Philippines had lost all eighteen of their B-17 bombers and fifty-five of their seventy-two P-40 fighter aircraft. The meaning was clear and simple to Douglas. In one swoop the Japanese had virtually wiped out American air power in the Philippines, dooming the country to certain invasion.

This fact was confirmed when Douglas learned that the only two Allied ships in the entire Western Pacific, the British battleship *Prince of Wales* and battle cruiser *Repulse*, had both been sunk off the coast of Malaya. The American submarines in the area had been ordered to retreat to Australia. The navy had abandoned the Philippines to invasion.

Two days later reports reached Douglas that Japanese troops were landing on the island of Luzon, at Aparri on the northern tip and at Vigan on the northwestern shore. Douglas was certain that these landings were a trap to lure American and Filipino troops away from the Manila area, where he felt the main attack would come.

Sure enough, on December 22, 1941, three days before Christmas, eighty Japanese ships sailed into the Lingayen Gulf north of Manila and landed troops at three points around the gulf, only one of which was defended by American and Filipino troops. The forty thousand Japanese soldiers who came ashore soon overwhelmed Douglas's troops, and many Filipino soldiers, who were not yet properly trained or battle tested, threw down their antiquated rifles and fled into the hills. This left a clear path of one hundred miles to Manila. The only obstacle in the Japanese path was the numerous rivers and creeks that crisscrossed the plain north of the city.

To make matters worse, Douglas received word that ten thousand more Japanese soldiers had landed around Lamon Bay, only sixty miles southeast of Manila. They had already formed themselves into three columns and were marching toward the capital. Within forty-eight hours the Japanese would have Manila in a pincer grip.

Douglas realized that the situation was hopeless, and he knew that the army had to fall back to the Bataan peninsula and Corregidor island in Manila Bay. He had surveyed this area on his previous postings to the Philippines and felt that the rugged, jungle-covered Bataan peninsula was the best place from which to mount a counterattack. The question became how to get the troops to the peninsula with minimal loss of life. Douglas soon came up with a plan. He ordered his troops to resist the Japanese march on Manila as fiercely as possible but avoid being encircled by the superior Japanese force and taken prisoner. Instead they were to fall back toward the Bataan peninsula, destroying every bridge they crossed and creating roadblocks at every turn to slow down the Japanese advance.

That is just what the troops did. American and Filipino soldiers fought ferociously side by side, falling back when the Japanese threatened to overrun them. And as they fell back, soldiers would rig the bridges with dynamite and destroy them. In this way they managed to slow the Japanese advance on Manila, but Douglas knew that the capture of the city was inevitable, and he made plans to evacuate it.

On December 24 Douglas sent his former naval adviser, Lieutenant Colonel Sidney Huff, to bring Jean, Arthur, and Arthur's Chinese nanny, Ah Cheu, to the dock at Manila Bay. By midafternoon the Manila skyline was a smoky haze as Japanese planes swooped down and bombed the city. Douglas drove his Packard motorcar to the dock, where he met up with his family. Three-year-old Arthur clung to his stuffed rabbit, and Ah Cheu held his new red tricycle, a Christmas gift that he had opened early. The family, like all of the people evacuating to Corregidor, had two bags of belongings among them. Jean told Douglas that she had packed a change of clothes for him, a photo of his parents, and some of his medals. Everything else had been left in the penthouse apartment, except for his father's collection of four thousand books, which were stored in an army warehouse. One of Douglas's last orders before leaving his office was to blow up all the warehouses and storerooms in Manila so that the Japanese would not be able to use American food and ammunition to bolster their own supplies. Douglas realized that his father's wonderful collection of books would be nothing but ashes by now.

As the MacArthurs stood waiting for the small interisland steamer that would ferry them to

Corregidor, Douglas noticed how calm and collected Jean was. It was a trait he admired greatly in her, and he was thankful that she was by his side.

Among the crowd of other people waiting to evacuate to Corregidor was President Quezon and his wife and family. They were leaving Manila along with most of the other members of the Philippine commonwealth government.

As dusk approached, the *Don Esteban* finally steamed up and moored alongside the dock. At the same time a convoy of heavily guarded trucks pulled up at the dock. President Quezon took Douglas aside and told him that the trucks carried all of the Philippines' gold and silver bullion reserves. It took over an hour to load it all onto the steamer, but eventually they cast off and headed out across Manila Bay. It was a balmy, moonlit night, and Douglas stood on deck looking back at the capital city. An eerie red glow radiated from the Pandacan oil fields, which had been one of the first Japanese targets to bomb.

Twenty-six miles from Manila, in the mouth of Manila Bay and two miles off the Bataan peninsula, the tadpole-shaped island of Corregidor came into view. The island covered three and a half square miles and at its highest point was 450 feet above sea level. Soon Douglas was walking briskly across the island toward the fortifications the Americans had built on the island. He and his family spent their first night on Corregidor in the confines of Malinta Tunnel. The tunnel was twelve feet high, thirty-five feet wide, and one hundred feet long.

Branching off from the main tunnel were smaller tunnels that housed a hospital, barracks, a communications post, and Douglas's cramped command center. The tunnel could also serve as a bomb shelter during air raids.

Douglas did not like being cooped up in the dank tunnel, and over the protests of his aides, the following morning he and his family took up residence in a small cottage high on the island.

Three days after arriving on Corregidor, Douglas organized for a campaign of guerrilla warfare to be waged against the Japanese in the central and southern islands of the Philippines. Then he turned his attention to defending the Bataan peninsula.

By New Year's Day 1942 eighty thousand American and Filipino troops had successfully retreated onto the peninsula. Douglas then ordered his commanding officers to form a defensive line across the neck of the Bataan peninsula where the American and Filipino troops would make their stand against the advancing Japanese.

Meanwhile the Japanese had captured Manila and soon learned that Douglas MacArthur had fled to Corregidor with nine thousand troops. The next day Japanese Mitsubishi dive-bombers swooped in on the island, bombarding it mercilessly. Anti-aircraft fire from Corregidor peppered the sky, trying to bring down the bombers. While those not manning the antiaircraft guns fled for cover in and around Malinta Tunnel, Douglas stood by a hedge to view the action. His aides begged him to seek cover, but Douglas explained to them that he wanted to see firsthand how the enemy was conducting the battle. He also believed passionately that a good military leader should be seen by his men taking the same risks that they had been ordered to take. It was how he had commanded his troops in France during the Great War, and he did not intend to change now.

After three hours the Japanese broke off the attack and the antiaircraft guns fell silent. Douglas surveyed the scene: buildings were battered and smashed, and the ground was pockmarked with small craters made by the Japanese bombs.

At exactly the same time the following day, more Mitsubishi dive-bombers arrived over Corregidor and bombed the American fortifications. After three hours they broke off the attack. The next day they did the same, and each day after that, until Douglas could set his watch by the arrival of the Japanese bombers.

As the siege of Corregidor went on, Douglas sent cable after cable to Washington, begging for reinforcements and supplies to be sent to his beleaguered troops. The replies urged him to continue his resistance, but they did not mention the men or supplies he desperately needed. It soon became obvious to Douglas that the United States government was focusing its attention, men, and supplies on the war in Europe and that his pleas for reinforcements were falling on deaf ears. As supplies of food and antiaircraft shells ran dangerously low, Douglas redoubled his efforts with Washington. Finally he received cables from President Roosevelt and the War Department promising that men and supplies were finally on their way. But as the days dragged on, no convoy of ships bearing the reinforcements of supplies emerged over the horizon.

It soon seemed to President Quezon that the United States had abandoned the Philippines, and Douglas found himself having to quell his old friend's anger and frustration, promising that America would come to their aid and that Filipino troops were not dying in vain. Yet Douglas himself could not help feeling abandoned, and his anger and frustration, especially with the War Department, grew.

With the food supplies running so low, food rations were cut in half and then in half again, until the men were surviving on fewer than one thousand calories a day. And with the shortage of shells, the antiaircraft guns no longer fired when the Japanese bombers flew in with their deadly cargo each morning. Things were beginning to get desperate on Corregidor.

The Bataan peninsula was no better off. Wave after wave of Japanese attacks had slammed into the American line there. The American and Filipino soldiers manning the line fought valiantly, inflicting heavy casualties on the Japanese and beating back their attack time after time. But the Japanese had one advantage Douglas did not have: they were continually being resupplied with food and ammunition and new recruits to replace those killed and wounded in battle. Eventually the American troops fell back to their secondary line of defense across the peninsula. The men were becoming weak from lack of food, and some of the soldiers had resorted to eating leaves, roots, and monkeys to stay alive. The sickly men fell victim to diseases such as malaria, dysentery, beriberi, and dengue fever.

Douglas made a trip across to the Bataan peninsula to encourage his men and urge them to keep fighting. By now the restricted rations were having an effect on him. He had lost twenty-five pounds, and his normally crisp uniform hung baggily on him, and his hair was long and scraggly.

Back on Corregidor, Douglas was surprised to receive a communiqué from Lieutenant General Masaharu Homma, commander of the Japanese forces in the Philippines. To his surprise Douglas learned that Homma had written the letter from Douglas's own penthouse apartment at the Manila Hotel:

To: General Douglas MacArthur
Commander in Chief
United States Army Forces in the Far East

Sir:

You are well aware that you are doomed. The end is near. The question is how long you will be able to resist. You have already cut rations by half. I appreciate the fighting spirit of yourself and your troops who have been fighting with courage. Your prestige and honor have been upheld.

However, in order to avoid needless bloodshed and to save the remnants of your divisions and your auxiliary troops, you are advised to surrender.

In the meantime, we shall continue our offensive as I do not wish to give you time for defense. If you decide to comply with our advice, send a mission as soon as possible to our front lines. We shall then cease fire and negotiate an armistice. Failing that, our offensive will be continued with inexorable force which will bring upon you only disaster.

Hoping your wise counsel will so prevail that you will save the lives of your troops, I remain,

Yours very sincerely,
General Masaharu Homma
Commander in Chief
The Japanese Expeditionary Force

Of course there was no way Douglas MacArthur was going to surrender. Even though he knew that the situation he and his men faced was overwhelming, given the physical state of his men, and even if no reinforcements arrived, he and his men would sooner die defending the Bataan peninsula and Corregidor island than surrender to the Japanese. Besides, their determined stand on the Bataan peninsula had slowed the Japanese advance through the Philippines to a crawl. And since Douglas believed that Japan wanted to use the Philippines as a stepping-stone to invading the whole western Pacific region, he figured their resistance was throwing off the whole Japanese timetable for invasion.

Douglas sent a message to President Roosevelt, informing him of his determination to fight to the bitter end rather than face surrender. "I intend to fight to destruction on Bataan and then do the same on Corregidor," part of his message read.

The withering bombing of Corregidor island continued day in and day out, and conditions on the island became desperate. Not a building on the island was left intact, which meant that more and more men were crowded into Malinta Tunnel. Despite the conditions, Douglas did his best to keep up the morale of his men. Each day he visited the sick and wounded in the underground hospital, and he was always visible, standing with his men during the daily Japanese bombing raids on the island. He was humbled to learn that the troops on the Bataan peninsula, despite the deplorable conditions they faced, were still holding out against the Japanese.

All the while Douglas hoped and prayed that supplies and reinforcements would soon arrive. A small freighter did manage to run the Japanese naval blockade of Manila Bay and make it to Corregidor, where it delivered a thousand tons of food. Douglas appreciated the captain's bravery in risking his ship and running the blockade, but the food was only enough to feed his men for four days.

In mid-February Douglas received word from Washington. Given the desperate situation on Corregidor island and on the Bataan peninsula, the navy was sending a submarine to evacuate President Quezon and his family and other members of the Philippine government on the island, as well as Jean and little Arthur. Douglas breathed a sigh of relief. President Quezon was in poor health with tuberculosis, and while Douglas was prepared to die fighting the Japanese on Corregidor, he did not want Jean and Arthur to have to suffer the same fate. He eagerly awaited the arrival of the submarine that would ferry his family to safety.

Chapter 11

Escape from Corregidor

On February 20, 1942, the Quezon family left for Australia aboard the American submarine *Swordfish*. Douglas had hoped that his wife and son would go with them, but Jean refused to leave him. She told him that she and Arthur would stay with him until the end and share in his fate, whatever that might be.

The last thing President Quezon did before leaving was to slip his signet ring onto Douglas's finger. "When they find your body, I want them to know you fought for my country," the president said.

Douglas fought back tears as he embraced his old friend.

The following day, which happened to be Arthur's fourth birthday, Douglas received a coded radio message from President Roosevelt ordering him to leave Corregidor and head south for Mindanao. There he was to see what could be done to shore up American defenses, and then he was to proceed to Australia, where he was to take up the role of commander of the newly formed Southwest Pacific Area.

Douglas was aghast at the idea of leaving his troops, and immediately he wired a message back to Washington.

> Please be guided by me in this matter [of when I should leave]. I know the situation here in the Philippines and unless the right moment is chosen for so delicate an operation, a sudden collapse might result. These people are depending upon me now...and any idea that might develop in their minds that I was being withdrawn for any other reason than to bring them immediate relief could not be explained.

President Roosevelt granted Douglas a little more time, but on March 10 the final order came. Douglas was to report to his new post in Melbourne, Australia, as soon as possible.

The first thing Douglas had to do was decide when and how he was going to flee Corregidor. At first he thought he would escape by submarine, as the Quezons and other important government leaders had. But when he learned that news of his pending escape had been talked about publicly in the United States and that Japanese spies had picked up on the story, he decided he needed a new plan. He thought of the four PT boats stationed on the Bataan peninsula. The boats were under the command of Lieutenant John Bulkeley. They were seventy-seven feet long, their hulls were made of mahogany, and their large Packard engines could push them along at a top speed of forty-five knots (or fifty-two miles per hour). They were armed with four torpedo tubes and four .50-caliber machine guns. The four boats were all that was left of a larger fleet of PT boats stationed out of Manila. Douglas decided that he would use these boats to make his escape.

The next thing he needed to decide was who to take with him. In his new post as commander of the Southwest Pacific Area, he would need some of his key staff aides. In the end Douglas chose his chief of staff, General Richard Sutherland, and fifteen other officers, along with his sergeant secretary. And of course Jean, Arthur, and Ah Cheu, Arthur's nanny, would be going with them.

A definite plan of escape was soon put in place. From Corregidor the PT boats would make their way through the minefield that guarded the entrance to Manila Bay. Then they would speed southward to Cagayan, 550 miles away on the north coast of the southern Philippine island of Mindanao. They would have to cover this distance without being spotted by the many Japanese warships that patrolled the west coast of the Philippines. It was a daring plan, and Douglas was aware of the risks and dangers involved. He knew that the plan had only a one-in-five chance of succeeding. But he was under orders from President Roosevelt, and if there was a chance they could make it, he would try.

Sunset on Wednesday, March 11, 1942, was set as the time and date for Douglas's departure from Corregidor. In preparation for his leaving, Douglas sent for General Jonathan Wainwright, his field commander leading the troops on the Bataan peninsula.

When General Wainwright arrived on Corregidor, Douglas explained that he was handing command of all the troops on Corregidor island and the Bataan peninsula over to him. Douglas's last words to General Wainwright before leaving were, "Jim, hold on till I come back for you."

At 7:15 in the evening PT-41, commanded by Lieutenant Bulkeley, pulled up to the bomb-ravaged south dock on Corregidor island. Douglas, Jean, Arthur, and Ah Cheu made their way to the dock. It was time to depart. Each person was allowed one bag weighing no more than thirty pounds to take with him or her. Douglas took nothing, not even his razor; he planned to borrow the lieutenant's. After Jean, Arthur, and Ah Cheu were safely aboard the boat, Douglas turned and looked out across Corregidor. The Japanese had turned the island into a living hell. Every plant, tree, and flower had been destroyed by the bombs, as had every building. Smoke and flames still belched from the remains of some of the buildings, and the ground everywhere was blistered by the pockmarks of Japanese bombs. It was a dismal sight, yet the bravest of the brave

American and Filipino troops still held the island and the peninsula beyond against a superior Japanese force. Tears filled Douglas's eyes as he thought of the destiny of all those men. *When I get to Australia,* he told himself, *I will return with an overwhelming force of fresh American soldiers, and we will take back the Philippines.* Douglas lifted his cap from his head as a final good-bye to his troops. Mechanically he turned and climbed aboard PT-41. "You may cast off, Buck, when you are ready," he told Lieutenant Bulkeley.

The big engines of the boat roared to life, and PT-41 headed away from Corregidor island. In the entrance to Manila Bay, they rendezvoused with PT boats 32, 34, and 35, which had picked up the other men departing Corregidor. The boats formed a line one after the other and made their way gingerly through the minefield at the entrance to Manila Bay. By now it was completely dark, and to avoid detection by the Japanese, every light on the boats had been turned off.

Once they cleared the minefield, the boats got into a diamond formation, with PT-41 leading the way. The diamond formation allowed the boats to fire their torpedoes at Japanese ships, if any gave chase, without hitting any of the other PT boats. However, the engines were badly in need of maintenance, and there had been no facilities to do this on Corregidor or Bataan. So they coughed and spluttered and could only be coaxed into going at half speed.

Furthermore, the noise of the engines on the boats was deafening, and the wind had come up, churning the ocean. The vessels jolted, pitched, and rolled wildly in the rough sea. Soon Arthur and Ah Cheu were lying seasick on the two officers' bunks below deck. Before long Douglas felt queasy himself and had to sprawl out on a mattress below deck. The boats plowed on until suddenly in the darkness they spotted several Japanese destroyers. They waited for the vessels to open fire on their position, but the enemy ships apparently had not spotted the PT boats. Lieutenant Bulkeley ordered the boats to change course, and they made their way farther west around the Japanese warships.

Before long they were battling eighteen- to twenty-foot-high waves. The PT boats creaked and moaned as they pummeled their way through the waves. It was a bruising, bone-jarring experience for everyone on board. Finally, at three thirty in the morning, the PT boats could hold formation no longer. The conditions were too bad. Salt spray whipped over PT-41, stinging the faces of all on deck and completely drenching everyone.

The original escape plan called for the PT boats to make it as far as the uninhabited Cuyo Islands by sunrise, where they would camouflage the boats and wait for sunset before setting out on the final leg of the journey to Cagayan. But the weather conditions would not let them do this. The boats were out of formation and had drifted apart, and as the sun came up, PT-41 took shelter at another uninhabited island three hours from the Cuyo Islands.

In a small cove on the island, they saw in the distance one of the other PT boats taking shelter, and they headed toward it. But the other PT boat thought they were an approaching Japanese patrol vessel and loaded their torpedoes, dumped the extra barrels of fuel overboard to lighten their load, and prepared to fight. It was only at the last minute that they realized what they thought was a Japanese patrol boat was actually PT-41, and they broke off their attack seconds before launching their torpedoes. By now, however, the drums carrying the extra fuel that PT-32 needed to make it all the way to Mindanao were at the bottom of the ocean.

The boats waited in the cove until two thirty in the afternoon, when the men decided to make a run for the Cuyo Islands in daylight. They set out as fast as the boats could ferry them through the still-turbulent ocean. At one point a Japanese destroyer seemed to appear out of nowhere in front of them, and the men were sure that they would be attacked. But somehow the boats remained unnoticed as they bobbed up and down between the mountainous waves, and the destroyer steamed on. Finally they made it to their original rendezvous point, where they found PT-34 waiting for them. But PT-35 was nowhere to be found. They waited at the rendezvous point until six thirty in the evening, when they divided those on board PT-32 between the other two boats. Since PT-32 no longer had any fuel, it had to be left behind. With the extra passengers aboard, PT boats 41 and 34 set out for Cagayan.

Once again they had to avoid Japanese naval vessels and endure rough seas, but at daybreak the north coast of the island of Mindanao was clearly visible before them. Douglas and everyone else on board breathed a sigh of relief when they finally made it to Cagayan at seven in the morning. They had beaten the odds so far. They had had only a small chance of making it to this point, and they had made it. PT-35, they learned later, had encountered engine trouble and as a result was many hours behind them. But it, too, eventually made it to Mindanao island, crowning the success of the mission.

Waiting at the dock to greet Douglas was Brigadier General William F. Sharp, who commanded the Visayan-Mindanao force. But before he stepped ashore at Cagayan, Douglas turned to the crews of the PT boats and said, "It was done in true naval style. It gives me great pleasure and honor to award the boats' crews the Silver Star for gallantry for fortitude in the face of heavy odds."

Once ashore Douglas learned from General Sharp that four B-17 aircraft had been sent from Australia to airlift them out of Mindanao. However, two of the planes never made it to Cagayan, probably shot down by Japanese planes, and one crashed offshore before landing. The fourth plane did get through but was in such a state of disrepair that General Sharp had sent it straight back to Australia empty and ordered three more aircraft to be sent.

It was two and a half days before the replacement airplanes were to arrive, and in that time Douglas rested and conferred with General Sharp. The general commanded twenty-five thousand troops on Mindanao and another twenty thousand

Filipino troops in the Visayans (central Philippines). His troops were waging a guerrilla war against the Japanese, who controlled the city of Davao and the south portion of Mindanao. It was agreed that if the men on Bataan and Corregidor could not hold out, General Sharp was to increase the scope of his guerrilla war against the Japanese.

Finally, at 8:00 PM on Monday, March 16, two of the three B-17 airplanes ordered by General Sharp to carry Douglas and his staff to Australia arrived at an airstrip that served the Del Monte plantation. As it turned out, these two airplanes were in not much better condition than the plane General Sharp had sent back empty. Regardless of their condition, the planes had made it there from Australia, and Douglas was sure that they could make it back. So with Arthur, who was still sick from the sea voyage, in his arms, Douglas, along with Jean and Ah Cheu, climbed aboard the first airplane, which within minutes was airborne.

As they headed south, they were flying over enemy territory, but under the cover of darkness they went undetected by the Japanese until they were over the island of Timor in the Dutch East Indies. There the Japanese spotted them, and Zero fighters were sent to intercept Douglas's plane. The pilot of the B-17 quickly changed course, and the Japanese fighters were unable to find the plane in the sky.

Finally, at 9:00 AM on March 17, six days after Douglas had left Corregidor, the plane carrying Douglas and his family touched down at Batchelor

Field, forty miles south of Darwin in northern Australia. The plane was supposed to have landed at the airport in Darwin, but it had received a radio message that the airport was under attack by Japanese bombers, and so it had diverted to Batchelor Field.

As soon as the doors of the B-17 swung open, Douglas climbed down onto the tarmac and found the nearest American officer. "How many American troops have been built up in Australia to retake the Philippines?" he asked.

The officer looked confused. "Not many, sir," he replied. "I don't think there is any plan in action for that."

Douglas was dumbfounded. He turned to his chief of staff, Richard Sutherland. "Surely he's wrong," he said.

Douglas and his family and staff spent only a few minutes on the ground at Batchelor Field before they climbed into another airplane for a flight to Alice Springs in the center of Australia. Douglas and Jean were still finding their seats when all of a sudden the engines of the plane revved loudly and the aircraft sped off down the runway, leaving Douglas and Jean sprawled on the floor. At first Douglas was angry with the pilot, but then he learned that the pilot had been alerted that Japanese bombers were on their way to bomb Batchelor Field. As a result of the pilot's quick actions, they had made it off the ground with only minutes to spare.

It was a three-hour flight to Alice Springs, and when they climbed out of the plane, Jean refused to get into another one. She had been cooped up on a boat and airplane long enough. From Alice Springs they were going to take the train south to Adelaide and then on to Melbourne. And that is what they did.

As they rumbled through the barren Australian outback, Douglas waited anxiously for news of a vast American buildup in Australia. But when he reached Melbourne, he found out the sobering truth. There were fewer than twenty-five thousand members of the American army and air force in the country, and most of them were engineers and support troops. On paper 250 airplanes were available, but few of them were fit to fly. Douglas felt physically ill as he realized that he would not be able to fulfill his promise and return to liberate the Bataan peninsula and Corregidor island anytime soon.

Douglas knew that given the present circumstances, defending Australia would take all of his men and skill. The Japanese were advancing southward through the Pacific islands at a relentless pace. They had taken Borneo, the Celebes Islands, Malaya, Java, and Timor and had just invaded the Solomon Islands. These occupations threatened not only Australia but also the Allied sea lanes from Hawaii across the western Pacific Ocean.

As if the lack of American troops were not enough, Douglas soon learned that most of the Australian army had been sent off to fight the Germans in Egypt and the Middle East. And having just traveled through the center of Australia, Douglas was acutely aware of the vast size of the country. It was roughly the same size as the United States, and Douglas was expected to take command and protect the country's entire shoreline from enemy attack.

That night Douglas did not sleep. He paced the floor, wondering whether he had been given an impossible task.

When Douglas's train reached Adelaide in South Australia on March 20, reporters were lined up at the station to see the new commanding officer of the American forces. They peppered him with questions, and Douglas referred to a few words he had scribbled on the back of an envelope in case the occasion arose.

"The President of the United States ordered me to break through the Japanese lines and proceed from Corregidor to Australia for the purpose, as I understand it, of organizing the American offensive against Japan, a primary object of which is the relief of the Philippines. I came through, and *I shall return*," he said.

Little did Douglas know that as these words were reported around the world, his last phrase, "I shall return," became a rallying cry, and no more so than to the Filipinos suffering under Japanese occupation.

Chapter 12

Island by Island

On March 26, 1942, Douglas MacArthur attended a dinner given in his honor by the Australian prime minister, John Curtin. After the meal Douglas was awarded the Medal of Honor, the highest award for valor in action against an enemy force that could be bestowed on an individual serving in the United States military. It was a sobering moment for Douglas as the medal was pinned on his uniform. He recalled his father receiving the same honor, and he knew that they were the only father and son to have ever both received the medal. Throughout the evening he also thought about the plight of the men left on Bataan and Corregidor. While he ate roast lamb and mashed potatoes, he knew that his men must have been running out of food and ammunition by then. How Douglas wished he could be with them. As he stood to speak, all of these thoughts surged through his mind.

"My faith in our ultimate victory is invincible," he began, "and I bring you tonight the unbreakable spirit of the free man's military code in support of our joint cause. There can be no compromise. We shall win or we shall die, and to this end I pledge the full resources of all the mighty power of my country and all the blood of my countrymen." Douglas looked down at the medal on his chest and then added, "This medal was intended not so much for me personally as it is a recognition of the indomitable courage of the gallant army which it was my honor to command."

The next day Douglas met with Prime Minister Curtin to make plans for the defense of Australia. By now Douglas realized that the rapid Japanese advance across the Pacific had demoralized Australia's seven million inhabitants. And everyone in the country knew what was supposed to happen when the Japanese invasion of Australia began. The government had drawn a line from Brisbane on the coast of Queensland in the east to Perth on the coast of western Australia. This line, dubbed the Brisbane Line, was the line that the Japanese invaders would be allowed to advance to while the Australians vigorously defended the area south of the line. All industrial plants and utilities north of the line would be blown up and ports dynamited so that the Japanese could not use them to support large ships.

The plan appalled Douglas. He had seen firsthand that the Japanese strength was in being on the offensive. When they attacked, they were nearly impossible to defeat. The Australians, he was convinced, needed to mount a surprise attack on the Japanese before they reached the shores of Australia. The ideal spot for such an attack, Douglas concluded, was in New Guinea, the large island to the north of Australia. The Japanese had already occupied half of the island and were threatening to take it over completely. The Australians would defend their country not on the continent itself but on the island of New Guinea. The idea spread like wildfire through the local population, giving them hope that they could avoid invasion and even turn the tide of war against the Japanese.

Meanwhile Douglas kept his ears open for any news of his men on Corregidor and Bataan. The intelligence that came through was discouraging. As he had calculated, the soldiers were very near the end of their rations of food and medicine. Then on April 3 Douglas heard the worst possible news: the Japanese had begun a massive attack on the Bataan peninsula. By April 9 the troops there had surrendered. A few men had been able to make it across the two miles of shark-infested waters to Corregidor, where they were now helping with the defense of the island, which still continued to hold out against the Japanese. However, more than 11,000 American soldiers had been taken prisoner, and all but 1,700 of the 66,000 Filipino troops on Bataan had been captured. Douglas learned that the Japanese had marched the captured soldiers off to Camp O'Donnell, a former Philippine army training facility located ten miles north of Clark Field. The camp was designed to hold 9,000 people, but soon the Japanese had over 50,000 American and Filipino prisoners crammed into it. With little to eat and crammed into such close quarters, many more men fell victim to dysentery, dengue fever, malaria, and beriberi.

Douglas was horrified to learn of the brutality of the Japanese. On the march up the Bataan peninsula to Camp O'Donnell, over 650 American soldiers had died or been killed. And the news Douglas continued to get was even grimmer. During the forty days the American soldiers were held at Camp O'Donnell before being moved elsewhere, another 1,500 of them died. Eventually, more than 25,000 Filipinos would die at Camp O'Donnell.

On May 6 Douglas received the news that Corregidor had finally fallen. The island had been relentlessly battered by shelling from the Bataan peninsula and from aerial bombardment, and with their supplies exhausted, General Wainwright had surrendered in the hope of avoiding a bloodbath on the island as the Japanese stormed it. The surrendered American soldiers were eventually transferred to a prison camp at Cabanatuan, located on the central plain of the island of Luzon.

Douglas felt saddened but proud when he heard the news. The men had fought gallantly, giving every ounce of their strength. But now it was over for them, and they faced an uncertain future at the hands of the Japanese. How he wished he had the manpower to march right back into the Philippines and take back the country from the Japanese and liberate the brave men of Bataan and Corregidor. Despite his personal feelings, Douglas knew that that would have to come later.

In the meantime Douglas had other troubles to deal with. He was trying desperately to draw more attention to the war in the Pacific, but President Roosevelt and British Prime Minister Winston Churchill were preoccupied with what was happening in Europe and the Middle East. When Douglas requested that two Australian military units be brought home to mount the offensive in New Guinea, Churchill replied that he believed that Japan was going to invade India next and that all Australian troops should be sent there.

A tussle over who had authority to order troop movement followed, a tussle that Douglas eventually won, and the Australian troops came home. Since these troops had been trained to fight in the desert, Douglas set them a rigorous schedule of training for jungle warfare. These Australian troops were bolstered by the arrival of the 32nd and 41st U.S. Infantry Divisions.

While the troops trained, Douglas moved his command headquarters from Melbourne to Brisbane.

In early June 1942 Douglas received some good news at last. The Americans had managed to break the Japanese codes and as a result had learned of a daring upcoming raid on the island of Midway in the North Pacific, close to the Hawaiian Islands. The Japanese were obviously planning to capture

Midway and use it as a stepping-off point for an invasion of Hawaii. However, when the Japanese fleet arrived at the island, they found a U.S. naval task force waiting for them. In the battle that followed, the Japanese navy was beaten, losing four aircraft carriers, two heavy cruisers, three destroyers, and two hundred seventy airplanes in the process. Douglas was delighted by the news. Despite their loss in the North Pacific, however, the Japanese still appeared to be fixated on invading Australia.

The Japanese had built bases on the northern coast of New Guinea, but Douglas reasoned that if they were to use the island as a jumping-off point for an invasion of Australia, the Japanese would need to capture Port Moresby. Port Moresby was the largest city in New Guinea, located on the southern side of the Papua peninsula at the eastern end of New Guinea. The city was only three hundred miles off Australia's northern coast and would put many other Australian cities within easy bombing range of Japanese bombers.

In late July Japanese forces landed on the north side of the Papua peninsula opposite Port Moresby and captured the towns of Buna and Gona. But between these towns and Port Moresby lay the formidable Owen Stanley Mountain Range. This range of high, razorback mountains, bisected by fast-flowing rivers and covered in impenetrable jungle, was virtually impossible to cross. As Douglas studied the map, he decided that from their beachhead at Buna and Gona, the Japanese would most likely land troops at Milne Bay at the eastern tip of the Papua peninsula, where they would bypass the Owen Stanley Range and have a clear run at Port Moresby. It was time to make a stand. Douglas dispatched the 7th Australian Division to Milne Bay to lie in wait for the Japanese.

Sure enough, eighteen days later, on August 7, 1942, a Japanese amphibious landing force surged into Milne Bay, only to be met by the deadly gunfire of the Australian troops. A pitched battle erupted, but the Australian forces won the day, and the Japanese were forced to retreat. It was the first time that a Japanese landing force had been repelled by Allied forces, and Douglas was determined it would not be the last.

Then to everyone's surprise, the Japanese sent fourteen thousand troops into the Owen Stanley Range, where they attempted to cross the mountains through the thirteen-thousand-foot-high Kokoda Pass. It seemed like a suicide mission, and the Japanese death toll was high, as exhausted men died from tropical diseases, fell to their deaths from the narrow slippery mountain trails, or were swallowed up by the bottomless quicksand pits along the way. The jungle they were passing through was so dense that it could take an hour's hacking with a machete to move a yard ahead. Nonetheless, waves of soldiers kept moving forward, inching their way closer to Port Moresby.

Again Douglas was determined to beat back the Japanese advance. He sent American and Australian troops to confront the Japanese. Upon confrontation, the Japanese soldiers did not put up much of a fight. They were too beaten down by the ordeal of crossing the Owen Stanley Range, and they soon turned and retreated back across the mountains, with Allied forces chasing them all the way. By the time they got back across the range, the Japanese soldiers were so hungry that they trampled over each other, leaving crushed comrades at the side of the trail as they made a mad dash for food at Buna and Gona.

With the success of his troops in New Guinea, on November 6 Douglas decided to move his forward command post to Port Moresby.

Meanwhile on Guadalcanal, in the neighboring Solomon Islands, U.S. marines had landed and were involved in a tenacious battle with the Japanese for control of that island.

Back in New Guinea, a small force of Americans made their way on foot over the Owen Stanley Range. Once on the north side of the Papua peninsula, they hacked several airstrips out of the dense jungle. As soon as the airstrips were complete, American planes ferried in American and Australian troops to begin an assault on the Japanese fortresses at Buna and Gona. With no naval ships available to open fire on the Japanese from the sea, the troops had to mount an all-out frontal attack on the Japanese positions. It was a grueling fight. Tropical diseases ravaged the troops, and the Japanese were well dug in and fought hard to defend their positions. But eventually the Allied forces prevailed, and on December 14 the fortress at Buna fell, as did the fortress at Gona five days later.

Douglas was delighted at the outcome. His forces had fought hard and valiantly, and he was particularly impressed with the fighting spirit of the Australian troops. But he knew it was only the beginning. Many more islands and Japanese strong-holds had to be overrun before the Japanese were vanquished.

As 1942 drew to a close, Douglas found his thoughts turning to Corregidor. It had been a year since he had fled to the island from Manila. He had hoped to be back in the Philippines by now, but things had not worked out that way. Yet he had not forgotten his promise. He *would* return and liberate the Philippines from the Japanese and free the brave soldiers from Bataan and Corregidor now wasting away in brutal Japanese prisoner-of-war camps.

In February 1943 Douglas received intelligence that a convoy of ships was about to transport a division of soldiers from the main Japanese base at Rabaul to the port of Lae on the north coast of New Guinea. Douglas and his commanders gambled that the convoy would pass through the Vitiaz Strait on its way to Lae, and there American fighters and bombers would intercept the ships. Sure enough, at 10:15 AM on the morning of March 3, 1943, the convoy was spotted sailing into the narrow strait. Within minutes American planes swarmed down on the convoy, dropping bombs and strafing the ships with machine-gun fire. When what became known as the Battle of the Bismarck Sea was over, six Japanese destroyers and fourteen merchant ships had been sunk, sixty Japanese airplanes had been shot down, and ten thousand Japanese troops had been lost at sea. The Americans had only thirteen men killed and twelve wounded; four planes had been shot down, and two more crashed while landing. It was a huge victory, and Douglas was encouraged by it.

Now Douglas turned his attention to winning Allied control of the sky over New Guinea. It took until the end of August for Allied aircraft to gain complete air supremacy. And when they had, Douglas turned his attention to overrunning the Japanese positions at Salamaua, Lae, and Finschhafen. By now Douglas had mustered enough craft to make an amphibious landing, and by using a combination of paratroopers and men landed amphibiously, his forces were able to encircle these strongholds and quickly overrun the Japanese positions. From victory here it was on to Wewak, farther west on the north coast of New Guinea, where once again the Japanese positions were overrun.

Feeling that he now had the upper hand in New Guinea, Douglas turned his attention to New Britain Island off the north coast of New Guinea, and in particular to Rabaul, the main supply base for the Japanese forces in the region. Rabaul was also an important air base out of which flew long-range Japanese bombers.

At Christmas 1943 Allied troops moved ashore at Arawe and then Cape Gloucester on the western tip of New Britain island and defeated the Japanese. At the same time, Allied bombers mercilessly pounded Rabaul from dawn to dusk, destroying the four

Japanese airfields there, sinking Japanese ships in the harbor, and destroying ammunition and supply dumps. This effectively cut the Japanese supply lines. At the same time, following victory at Guadalcanal, Admiral William Halsey, commander of the South Pacific theater of operations, was pushing northwest through the Solomon Islands. This operation, combined with Douglas's, left more than 150,000 Japanese troops stranded without ammunition, food, or reinforcements and effectively sidelined for the rest of the war.

After securing New Ireland, the long, narrow island to the northeast of New Britain, Douglas turned his attention to the Admiralty Islands to the west, and particularly to the island of Los Negros, with its airfield and natural harbor. With this strategic island captured, Douglas reasoned that the larger island of Manus would soon fall. However, Los Negros would not be easy to take. About four thousand Japanese soldiers were on the tiny island, and the operation would be taking place at the farthest extremity of the Allied supply line. To make matters more difficult, the number of Japanese troops on the island could be strengthened with troops from neighboring Manus. But during the course of his operations against the Japanese, Douglas felt he had come to understand how the mind of Japanese officers worked. He reasoned that, yes, more troops would be sent to Los Negros once the fighting began, but he was sure that the Japanese commanders would send them in small, ineffectual squads that could easily be defeated by the invading Allied forces.

Still, the whole operation was a gamble. It depended on Allied forces quickly capturing and securing the airfield on the island so that fresh supplies and reinforcements could be flown in. Given the risky nature of the operation, Douglas decided to accompany his troops into battle this time. He wanted to be there to personally issue the order to retreat if their gamble did not pay off.

On February 29, 1944, Douglas stood at the rail of the USS *Phoenix,* staring out at the island of Los Negros as the U.S. 1st Cavalry Division stormed ashore onto the island. The Japanese fought back, but despite the resistance, the American forces captured the beach and moved inland. Douglas himself was soon standing on the beach, congratulating his men. Then he strode inland toward the strategic airfield, ignoring the danger from Japanese snipers. He walked up and down the coral runway of the airfield, and when he was satisfied with its condition, he returned to the *Phoenix.* As Douglas had predicted, the Japanese commanders did send in small groups of reinforcements, who were easily defeated. When he was certain the situation on Los Negros was secure, he returned to his headquarters in Brisbane, Australia.

With the capture of Los Negros, the larger island of Manus soon capitulated, and the Admiralty Islands were now under Allied control. Douglas then focused attention back on New Guinea, capturing the important Japanese base at Hollandia, on the north coast of the island. Step by step Douglas was getting closer to his goal of liberating the Philippines.

On July 25, 1944, Douglas sat peering out the window of a B-17 bomber headed for Honolulu, Hawaii. In his breast pocket was a note that read, "Proceed to Pearl Harbor for meeting with Mr. Big, July 26. Top secret, no prior information will be given. Signed General G. Marshall, Joint Chiefs of Staff."

During the twenty-six-hour flight from Australia, Douglas had plenty of time to think about the possible meaning of the message. He had a hunch that Mr. Big was President Franklin Roosevelt, and he hoped that the meeting would be about the smartest way for Allied forces to attack Japan and end the war. Just a month and a half before, on June 6, a massive Allied force had stormed ashore on the beaches of Normandy, France, and were now beating back Hitler's troops. It was looking more and more like an end to the war in Europe was in sight. Now, Douglas predicted, the full force of the Allies would be brought to bear on the Pacific region.

Douglas felt hopeful as the B-17 circled Hickam Field and touched down on the hot tarmac. He was even more hopeful when orders awaited him on his arrival to proceed to the cruiser *Baltimore* in Pearl Harbor, where he would meet with President Roosevelt and Admirals Chester Nimitz and William Halsey. It seemed to Douglas that they were a group of leaders who could hurry along his plan to retake the Philippines and use those islands as a base to invade Japan and force its surrender.

A huge cheer went up from the crew of the *Baltimore* as Douglas strode up the gangplank and into the stateroom where the president, the two admirals, and several others had gathered. Douglas saluted the president and hoped that the shock he felt at the condition of Franklin Roosevelt did not show on his face. The fact was that the president, who was up for reelection for a fourth term, was in very poor health. In the seven years since Douglas had last seen him, he had seemingly aged twenty years. Douglas wondered how long the president had to live.

Even though Roosevelt's body was frail, Douglas was impressed with the president's grasp of the situation. Over the next two days, the small group of men looked at their options for subduing Japan, which had proven to be a tenacious foe whose troops would rather fight to the death than be captured. There was no talk of an easy surrender. The Japanese would have to be beaten down so far that they could see absolutely no way to keep fighting. The question became how this was to be done.

Douglas argued that the Allies should first take back the Philippines. He felt that fewer troops would be lost if they used the Philippines as the staging point for an invasion of Japan. With the Allies holding the Philippines, the South China Sea would be sealed off so that the Japanese could not get supplies to and from the south. Douglas also argued forcefully that the United States had a moral obligation to liberate the Philippine Islands and the thousands of prisoners of war being held there.

On the other hand, Admiral Nimitz, representing the views of Admiral Ernest King, the commander in chief of the navy, felt that the Allies should take the island of Formosa, off the coast of China, which was occupied by the Japanese. The Allies could then use Formosa as a staging ground to hit Japan hard, and there were fewer occupied islands that would have to be taken along the way to the east of Formosa than there were to the south of the Philippines.

Douglas was not sure which way the president was leaning until right at the end of the talks. Just as Douglas was about to leave, Roosevelt called him over. "Well, Douglas," he said, "you win! But I am going to have a tough time over this with that old bear Ernie King!"

Nothing the president might have said could have pleased Douglas more. All the way back to Brisbane, Douglas pored over maps and planned his strategy. The way ahead was not easy. Several Japanese-occupied islands would have to be captured so that they could be used to launch American planes and ships toward the Philippines.

Back in Brisbane, Douglas soon received instructions from the Joint Chiefs of Staff in Washington, D.C. He was to capture the islands of Morotai and Palau around September 15, the Talauds on October 15, then Mindanao in the southern Philippines exactly a month after that, and finally Leyte on December 20. He set out to ready his troops for the campaign.

In an attempt to keep his troops' spirits from flagging, Douglas decided to accompany invasion forces to Morotai aboard the cruiser *Nashville.* All went as planned, and Douglas transferred to the first troop boat to hit the beach. The boat was grounded on a rock, and when he stepped off the ramp, Douglas discovered that the water was chest-deep, but that did not dampen his enthusiasm. There was even less opposition from the Japanese on Morotai than he had expected, and not a single Allied soldier lost his life in the fighting.

During the voyage to Morotai, the *Nashville* had observed radio silence to prevent detection by the enemy. When everyone was safely on the beach, radio contact was reestablished. The first message Douglas heard both elated and saddened him. The message was from the Joint Chiefs of Staff, and it said that new intelligence suggested that there would not be as much Japanese resistance on Leyte as first thought. Because of this, the Joint Chiefs had decided to scrap plans to invade the Talauds and Mindanao, and instead Douglas should mount a direct assault against Leyte, one of the central Philippine islands. The bad news was that this decision had come too late to recall the 1st Marine Division, which had been aboard a convoy headed for Palau under radio silence. In keeping with the original plan, the 1st Marine Division had stormed ashore at Palau, where they had waged a hard-fought battle for the island. Their victory had come at a high price: over nine thousand Americans had died storming the island.

After receiving the message, Douglas wanted to be alone to digest the information. He strolled along the shoreline of Morotai, looking north toward the

Philippines. Just three hundred miles away lay Leyte, and beyond that Manila, Bataan, and Corregidor. "They are waiting for me there," he said quietly under his breath. "It has been a long time."

Chapter 13

"I Have Returned"

A month later, on October 19, 1944, Douglas MacArthur stood on the bridge of the *Nashville* in the midst of one of the most powerful armadas ever assembled. Every type of American naval vessel was there—over seven hundred aircraft carriers, cruisers, destroyers, escorts, and landing craft. Between them they carried two hundred thousand men, ready to face the Japanese on the beaches of Leyte in the Philippine Islands.

For two days the fleet had plowed forward, evading torpedoes from Japanese submarines and waiting for the action to begin. Just before midnight the captain of the *Nashville* told Douglas that they were entering the Leyte Gulf. Douglas peered into the dark and moonless night, but he could not see anything. Anxiously he waited with the men for several hours, then retired to his cabin to read the Bible and pray for victory the following morning.

Although he did not tell those around him, Douglas was particularly concerned about one aspect of the upcoming invasion. The Joint Chiefs of Staff had insisted that the invasion be led not by one commander but by two. While Douglas was given control over the army troops, Admiral Halsey, who answered only to Admiral Nimitz in Hawaii, was in charge of the navy. Although Douglas had pressed the Joint Chiefs to appoint either him or Admiral Halsey as supreme commander, they would not do it for political reasons. Now, with the battle only hours away, Douglas prayed that the army and navy would work as one smooth unit, especially since the navy had to supply all of the air cover for his troops.

As the sun came up over the Philippine Islands the next morning, the boom of ships' guns rent the air. Whatever might happen, it was too late to turn back now. Douglas watched as the shells exploded beyond the palm trees that lined the beach, softening up the Japanese defenses. Then he saw something he had waited two and a half long years to see—the first wave of Allied landing barges headed toward the beach. The soldiers aboard the craft stormed ashore onto the beach. A second wave of landing barges set out for the beach. One thing Douglas noticed as he watched these craft make their way ashore was that the Japanese defenses were not nearly as light as intelligence had reported. Japanese aircraft were soon buzzing overhead, swooping in on the ships and men going ashore. Despite the increased resistance, it was time for Douglas MacArthur himself to go ashore.

Douglas climbed down a ladder over the side of the *Nashville* and stepped onto a landing barge. The barge then made its way to the transport ship *John Land*, where they took aboard Sergio Osmeña, the new president of the Philippines. Douglas's old friend Manuel Quezon had died in exile, and Osmeña had been sworn in to take his place. Until now, however, he had been president of nothing; Japan controlled his country. Today Osmeña was going to step back onto his country's soil as president.

After Osmeña was safely aboard, the landing barge turned and headed for the beach. Fifty yards from shore the barge ran aground, and Douglas had to wade ashore, just as he had on the island of Morotai. He strode through the water, and when he reached the beach he lit his pipe and began to inspect his troops. He made an easy target in his uniform, and several Japanese snipers aimed and fired at him. As bullets whizzed past him, Douglas did not even flinch. He stood his ground, waiting for his men to return fire.

Soon two flags were hoisted up coconut trees. One was the American flag, and the other the Filipino flag. It was an emotional moment as Douglas saluted them both.

By that time a mobile broadcasting unit had been set up, and an officer handed Douglas a microphone. His hands trembling with emotion, Douglas took it and started to speak.

"People of the Philippines," he began, "I have returned. By the grace of Almighty God, our forces stand again on Philippine soil—soil consecrated in the blood of our two peoples. We have come, dedicated and committed to the task of destroying every vestige of enemy control over your daily lives, and of restoring upon a foundation of indestructible strength the liberties of your people.... Rally to me. Let the indomitable spirit of Bataan and Corregidor lead on. As the lines of battle roll forward to bring you within the zone of operations, rise and strike. Strike at every favorable opportunity. For your homes and hearths, strike! For future generations of your sons and daughters, strike! In the name of your sacred dead, strike! Let no heart be faint. Let every arm be steeled. The guidance of Divine God points the way. Follow in His name to the Holy Grail of righteous victory."

When Douglas had finished addressing the Filipino people, he walked off the beach and into the surrounding bush. He found a log to sit on and pulled out his message pad and a pencil and began to compose a letter to Franklin Roosevelt.

Dear Mr. President,

This note is written from the beach near Tacloban where we have just landed. It will be the first letter from the freed Philippines. I thought you might like it for your philatelic collection. I hope it gets through.

The operation is going smoothly and if successful will strategically as well as tactically cut the enemy forces in two. Strategically it will pierce the center of his defensive line extending along the coast of Asia from the Japanese homeland to the tip of Singapore, and will enable us to envelop to the north or south as we desire.... Tactically it divides his forces in the Philippines in two and by bypassing the southern half of the Philippines will result in the saving of possibly fifty thousand American casualties.

Douglas went on to outline how he thought a national government could be reinstated in the country and ended the letter with, "Please excuse this scribble but at the moment I am on the combat line with no facilities except this field message pad."

That night Douglas returned to the *Nashville,* and the following morning he was awakened by the sound of fifty Japanese bombers overhead. He watched as the bombers pummeled the beach before eventually being turned back by American planes and ground fire.

The fighting continued on land and in the air until October 23, when American intelligence intercepted a coded Japanese message: "All forces will dash to the attack, trusting in divine assistance." The meaning was clear: the entire imperial Japanese navy was steaming toward a showdown in Leyte Gulf. Immediately Douglas brought his headquarters ashore so that the *Nashville* could prepare for the massive naval battle that was sure to follow.

The Japanese fleet descended on Leyte Gulf from Singapore and Japan. American warships destroyed one arm of their fleet as it attempted to pass through the narrow Surigao Strait. Another arm of the Japanese fleet was sent mostly as a decoy to draw Admiral Halsey's naval task force away from Leyte. The admiral took the bait and was soon steaming out to sea after the Japanese ships. A third arm of Japanese ships had attacked and then retreated. At least that is what the American commanders thought. But this arm of the Japanese fleet had left the battle only to regroup. Just as the American commanders were about to congratulate themselves for winning the battle, the Japanese navy swept in again. This time they aimed right at the ships protecting Douglas's landing on the shores of Leyte. These American ships were mostly destroyers and escorts, and they were not much against the mightier Japanese battleships descending upon them. If they broke through, these battleships with their eighteen-inch guns would be able to open fire upon Leyte and Douglas's troops and wipe them out.

The American ships put up a valiant fight, but it was obvious that the Japanese had won the battle and would soon move into position to start pounding the two hundred thousand soldiers who had gone ashore. But then, with Leyte in their sights, the Japanese vessels turned and retreated. Douglas could hardly believe it! Later the Americans intercepted a coded message in which the Japanese admiral explained to his superiors that he had retreated because he feared that a massive air attack from land was about to be launched against his ships and that Admiral Halsey and his task force were steaming at full speed toward the Leyte Gulf.

On Leyte, Douglas breathed a sigh of relief. The tide was turning, but there was still much to do. Although the Japanese had lost the battle for the sea, they had plenty of land bases in the Philippines from which to launch air and land attacks against the Allied forces. For the next two months the two sides fought hard for every inch of Leyte. Both sides brought in reinforcements, and it was not until December 26, 1944, that Douglas felt confident in his announcement that the island of Leyte, along with the island of Mindoro, was now entirely in Allied hands.

In human terms the cost had been high. Over 3,300 Americans had been killed in the fighting, and three times that many had been injured. The Japanese, Douglas soon learned, had fared much worse. They had refused to surrender, preferring to die for their emperor and the glory of their country. Because of this only 798 Japanese soldiers had been captured while over 80,000 of them had died on Leyte.

In the midst of the battle for Leyte that December, Douglas and three other army generals had been promoted to a newly created rank of general of the army, or five-star general. After the battle the Philippine government—or what little of it was represented in Leyte—presented Douglas with the Medal of Valor, but Douglas hardly had time to collect the honor. His mind was on one thing and one thing only—liberating the island of Luzon, and in doing so, taking back Manila, Corregidor island, and the Bataan peninsula.

This called for master planning, and Douglas set about deceiving the Japanese as never before. He planned to invade Luzon at the Lingayen Gulf on the western side of the island, as the Japanese had done when they invaded Luzon, while all making it seem as though they were going to attack the south at Legaspi and Batangas.

Douglas ordered American bombers to target the south of Luzon and made sure that reconnaissance airplanes would be spotted in the area. He also ordered PT boats to patrol the sea of southern Luzon and guerrillas to sabotage Japanese positions whenever possible. In the meantime he was planning a daring invasion at the Lingayen Gulf.

On January 4, 1945, a convoy sailed northward from Leyte. On the bridge of the light cruiser *Boise* stood Douglas, surveying the nearly 1,000 ships, 3,000 landing craft, and 280,000 men. The air crackled with tension. After thirty-seven months Americans were about to attempt to retake Luzon.

Even before they steamed close to land, Japanese planes spotted them, and a relentless air attack began. The Japanese, who had become increasingly desperate as Douglas's army surged northward, had a new fighting tactic. The pilots of the small Zero fighters were ordered to use their planes as weapons, flying them right into enemy ships in what soon became known as kamikaze, or suicide, raids. Douglas watched as the kamikaze pilots buzzed overhead, chose a target, and dove their aircraft into it. Enormous plumes of black smoke rose over oily seas as forty U.S. vessels were sunk in the attacks.

Still the *Boise* cut through the waves, and before dawn on Wednesday, January 10, it lay at anchor in the Lingayen Gulf off the town of Lingayen. As the sun came up, Douglas noted that the water was particularly calm, and many of the men took it as a sign that God was with them.

Sirens began to scream as four army divisions scrambled into landing craft and hit the beach. There was little opposition, and Douglas soon joined them ashore. The Americans pushed eight miles inland before the day was out. Douglas was satisfied, but now that they were ashore, he wanted to liberate the prisoners of war as soon as possible. He feared that since the Japanese were on the defensive, they would begin treating their prisoners more harshly with each passing day.

Douglas ordered attacks on Subic Bay, Olongapo, and Mariveles, at the tip of the Bataan peninsula. Each of these advances went smoothly, with little loss of American lives because the Japanese were quickly retreating to Baguio in the mountains in the center of Luzon.

Next Douglas set his sights on Corregidor. He landed a regiment of airborne troops on the height of the island, and infantry troops used landing craft to land on the beach. The fighting was intense, and

210 American soldiers were killed in the ten-day battle for control of the island. The battle ended when 1,500 Japanese troops retreated into a tunnel and blew themselves up.

Now that Corregidor was captured, Douglas was ready to take Manila. As he moved southward, thousands of Filipinos recognized his five-star insignia and mobbed his jeep. They reached out to kiss his hands, press wreaths around his neck, and decorate the jeep with flowers. It was a triumphant moment for Douglas, but one that was soon overshadowed by a long and bloody battle for the capital city.

With the invasion of Luzon by Allied forces and the retreat of the Japanese to Baguio, about thirty thousand Japanese sailors and marines were trapped defending Manila. However, they were not about to give up the city without a fight. As American troops advanced into the city, the surviving Japanese soldiers fell back into Manila's narrow streets. Finally they crowded into the old walled city of Intramuros, in the heart of Manila. Its four-century-old walls were forty feet thick and twenty-five feet high. There the Japanese made a last desperate stand, holding the American forces at bay for several weeks. Heavy guns were brought in to bombard the Japanese position. The shelling destroyed most of the buildings within the walls, and finally the wall was breached, and inch by inch the American forces took back the city.

In the course of the fighting, Manila had been laid waste. Seventy percent of the utilities had been destroyed, along with 75 percent of the factories and 80 percent of the residential district to the south, and the whole of the business district had been totally annihilated. The streets of the city ran with blood. Japanese soldiers had gone on a murderous rampage in Manila. Almost 100,000 residents of the city had been killed, and in the most brutal ways imaginable. It made Douglas sick to his stomach to see the atrocities the Japanese military had carried out in Manila. The exotic city that he so fondly remembered was now a horrific wasteland.

Amazingly, one of the few buildings in the city still standing relatively unscathed was Malacañan Palace, the official residence of the Philippine president. Here, on February 27, while American forces still fought to take back Intramuros, Douglas held a ceremony to formally restore the capital back to Sergio Osmeña. During the ceremony Douglas made a speech, declaring:

> More than three years have elapsed— years of bitterness, struggle, and sacrifice— since I withdrew our forces and installations from this beautiful city that, open and undefended, its churches, monuments, and cultural centers might, in accordance with the rules of warfare, be spared the violence of military ravage. The enemy would not have it so, and much that I sought to preserve has been unnecessarily destroyed by his desperate action at bay. By these actions he has wantonly fixed the future pattern of his own

doom.... On behalf of my government, I now solemnly declare, Mr. President, the full powers and responsibilities under the Constitution restored to the Commonwealth, whose seat is here reestablished as provided by law. Your country, thus, is again at liberty to pursue its destiny to an honored position in the family of free nations. Your capital city, cruelly punished though it be, has regained its rightful place—citadel of democracy in the East.

On April 12, as American forces were pursuing the last pockets of Japanese resistance in the Philippines, Douglas received the sad news that President Franklin Roosevelt had died. This did not surprise him, but the timing of the president's death dismayed him. Roosevelt had a broad understanding of the Allies' military objectives. Douglas wondered whether Roosevelt's successor, Harry S. Truman, who had just been sworn in to office, would demonstrate that same depth of understanding. And how would Douglas relate to this new commander in chief?

Less than a month after the death of Franklin Roosevelt, on May 8, 1945, news reached Douglas in the Philippines that Germany had surrendered. The war in Europe was finally over. Douglas was elated. It meant that more military resources could now be focused on the next big goal in the war in the Pacific—the defeat and capture of Japan. Douglas knew that this was not going to be an easy task, if the tenaciousness of the Japanese soldiers they had encountered all the way across the Pacific was anything to go by.

Indeed, the Americans already had a foretaste of what it was going to be like to invade Japan. On February 19, as Douglas's troops were struggling to retake Manila, U.S. marines had invaded the Japanese island of Iwo Jima. By the time the island was captured on March 16, more than four thousand American soldiers had been killed and over fifteen thousand wounded. And on April 1 American forces had invaded the southern Japanese island of Okinawa, and the casualty rate Douglas was hearing from that battle was horrendous.

Finally, on July 5, 1945, Douglas sent out a message that read: "The entire Philippine Islands is liberated.... The Japanese during the operation employed twenty-three divisions, all of which were practically annihilated. Our forces comprised seventeen divisions."

Japan was now the next and final target.

Chapter 14

Surrender

Douglas MacArthur was working hard in the Philippines to prepare his forces for the invasion of Japan when in late July a representative from the War Department in Washington called on him. Although the representative would not give any details, he warned Douglas not to put any troops in or around Hiroshima in the first two weeks of August because the United States was planning something "big."

The big event, Douglas soon found out, was the dropping of the newly developed atomic bomb. Along with the rest of the world, Douglas learned that a B-29 bomber had dropped the bomb on Hiroshima on August 6, and this was followed up with a second atomic bomb dropped on Nagasaki three days later. Together the two bombs killed

112,000 people and wounded 128,000. It was a terrible toll to extract from the Japanese people, but Douglas concurred with other military leaders that if it cowed the Japanese into surrender, it would save the lives of hundreds of thousands of Allied soldiers.

At the same time, Joseph Stalin, the Russian leader, declared war on Japan and began an assault on Manchuria, which the Japanese occupied. This, combined with the threat of another atomic bomb, finally drove the Japanese government to surrender on August 15. The government's only request was that the emperor, whom many Japanese people considered to be divine, be allowed to retain his title. This request was granted.

And so August 15, 1945, marked the end of fighting in World War II. For Douglas it meant something else as well. It was the day he received a telegram from President Truman appointing him the Supreme Commander for the Allied Powers in Japan. The exact directions from President Truman read, "From the moment of surrender the authority of the Emperor and Japanese Government to rule the state will be subject to you." Never before in the history of the United States had so much power been given to one person. In one move Douglas MacArthur had been given the powers and responsibilities that for generations had belonged only to the Japanese emperor.

It was a sobering day, and before it was over, Douglas was making plans to accept the final surrender of the Japanese aboard the battleship *Missouri* and take on his new role.

Douglas decided to make his appearance in Japan at Atsugi Air Force Base on the outskirts of Yokohama. Everyone he knew tried to talk Douglas out of doing this. Atsugi was the training base for the dreaded kamikaze pilots, many of whom still lived on or near the base. A group of these pilots had refused to accept the surrender and had invaded the imperial palace grounds in an attempt to assassinate the emperor. They had not been successful, but they had killed the commanding general of the imperial guard division and fired on the prime minister's house. However, Douglas felt that he understood the Japanese mindset and that now, with the surrender already in place, they would honor it.

Once again Douglas was taking a huge gamble—a gamble with his life. But he felt it was necessary to demonstrate to the Japanese people that he was not afraid of them.

At two o'clock on August 30, Douglas and a small contingent of American military officers arrived at Atsugi Air Force Base. They were unarmed and unescorted as they climbed out of the airplane. It was a somber moment for Douglas as he stood on Japanese soil. He remarked to the officer standing beside him, "Bob, from Melbourne to Tokyo is a long way, but this seems to be the end of the road."

The newly arrived contingent of American officers climbed into an array of dilapidated cars and set out on the fifteen-mile drive into Yokohama. All along their route were lines of armed Japanese soldiers. Each man stood at attention with his back to the procession. One of the Japanese men accompanying the American contingent explained that this was a sign of respect normally reserved for the emperor. In fact most Japanese had never seen the emperor because they had been taught that if their eyes met his, they would go blind or die.

As they drove through the streets of Yokohama, Douglas was struck by the utter desolation that Allied bombing had visited on the once-bustling city. Shop windows were boarded up, and the sidewalks deserted.

Finally the motorcade pulled up at the New Grand Hotel, where Douglas had decided to set up his initial headquarters. The officers accompanying him seemed relieved when they were eventually inside the building, but Douglas had not for a single minute worried about being fired on. Nor was he worried that night when the Japanese chef prepared a steak especially for him. One of Douglas's generals leaned over to him and whispered, "You're not going to eat that without having someone taste it for you, are you? It could well be poisoned."

Douglas laughed. "No one can live forever," he said as he cut himself off a hearty slice of the steak and began to chew it.

As Douglas sat eating dinner, the door to the dining room swung open and in walked a tall, gaunt, haggard man with sunken cheeks, using a cane to steady himself. Douglas rose to his feet immediately. He walked over to the man and embraced him. It was his old field commander from Bataan, Lieutenant General Jonathan Wainwright. Douglas barely recognized him. General Wainwright had always been skinny, but now his uniform was baggy and hung from him. As they sat and talked, General Wainwright described the surrender of Corregidor and how he had been taken to a Japanese prisoner-of-war camp near Mukden, in China's northern province of Manchuria. He told of the three years there and how he had anguished over surrendering his men to such a brutal enemy. Douglas listened with tears in his eyes.

As soon as Douglas had learned that the general was still alive, he had sent for him. He wanted his old friend to have a place of honor at the surrender ceremony. It would be a fitting end to his three years in captivity. He was glad that his old friend had made it in time.

Sunday, September 2, 1945, dawned a cool, gloomy day. Clouds hung low over Tokyo Bay. At anchor, eighteen miles out in the bay off Yokohama, sat the forty-five-thousand-ton battleship *Missouri.* Douglas was the first to admit that she was an impressive sight. From her mast a large American flag fluttered in the breeze, and row upon row of sailors dressed in crisp, white uniforms lined the decks and railing of the ship. Beyond the *Missouri* lay line after line of Allied war ships at anchor. Amid this impressive display of military power, the destroyer *Lansdown* made its way toward the *Missouri.* The destroyer carried the Japanese delegation that would formally sign the surrender documents.

Douglas was already aboard the *Missouri,* and he paced back and forth in a cabin below deck, eager for the ceremony to begin. Finally an aide told him the Japanese had arrived, and Douglas made his way to the quarterdeck, where the eleven members of the Japanese delegation were lined up in four rows facing a table. On the green cloth that covered the table sat two copies of the surrender document that they would sign. A scaffold had been erected on one side of the deck for reporters and cameramen to record the event. The scaffold was now filled to overflowing as men clung to it and craned their necks to get a better view of what was about to happen. On the other side of the deck stood rows of American officers in neatly pressed khaki uniforms. And all around, peering over rails, hanging from gun turrets, and standing anywhere else that afforded a view of the proceedings were sailors.

Douglas strode out onto the quarterdeck and took his place, standing on the opposite side of the table facing the Japanese. At his side and one step behind was Lieutenant General Wainwright, standing in the position of honor. Standing in a U shape behind Douglas were the Allied admirals and generals who would also affix their signatures to the surrender document.

The surrender ceremony then officially got under way. Douglas stepped up to a microphone and addressed the gathering:

> We are gathered here, representatives of the major warring powers, to conclude a solemn agreement whereby peace may be

restored. The issues, involving divergent ideals and ideologies, have been determined on the battlefields of the world and hence are not for our discussion or debate. Nor is it for us here to meet, representing as we do a majority of the people of the earth, in a spirit of distrust, malice or hatred. But rather it is for us, both victors and vanquished, to rise to that higher dignity which alone befits the sacred purposes we are about to serve, committing all our people unreservedly to faithful compliance with the obligation they are here formally to assume.

It is my earnest hope and indeed the hope of all mankind that from this solemn occasion a better world shall emerge out of the blood and carnage of the past—a world founded upon faith and understanding—a world dedicated to the dignity of man and the fulfillment of his most cherished wish—for freedom, tolerance and justice.

The terms and conditions upon which the surrender of the Japanese Imperial Forces is here to be given and accepted are contained in the instrument of surrender now before you.

As Supreme Commander for the Allied Powers, I announce it my firm purpose, in the tradition of the countries I represent, to proceed in the discharge of my responsibilities with justice and tolerance, while taking all necessary dispositions to ensure that the terms of surrender are fully, promptly and faithfully complied with.

When he was finished speaking, Douglas invited the two senior Japanese delegates, Foreign Minister Mamoru Shigemitsu, representing the government, and General Yoshijiro Umedzu, representing the Supreme Command, to step forward and sign the surrender document. Both men signed their names at the bottom of the document. With two strokes of a pen they ended the hostilities that had cost Japan the lives of 1,270,000 soldiers and 670,000 civilians.

Then, at eight minutes past nine in the morning, Douglas MacArthur stepped forward and put his signature on the document. The representatives of the Allied powers present then stepped forward and did the same. In all, representatives from the United States, China, Great Britain, the Soviet Union, Australia, Canada, France, the Netherlands, and New Zealand signed the surrender document.

When these representatives had finished affixing their signatures, Douglas said, "Let us pray that peace be now restored to the world and that God will preserve it always. These proceedings are closed."

As he said these words, much to everyone's amazement, the sun broke through the clouds and shined brightly on the *Missouri.* As the participants in the ceremony stood basking in the sun, a thunderous roar suddenly filled the sky as four hundred B-29 bombers and fifteen hundred aircraft carrier planes flew overhead as a final salute. All aboard the *Missouri* stood at attention, and then the official ceremony was over. World War II had finally ended.

Following the ceremony, Douglas broadcast a message to the American public:

> Today the guns are silent. A great tragedy has ended. A great victory has been won. The skies no longer rain death—the seas bear only commerce—men everywhere walk upright in the sunlight. The entire world is quietly at peace. The holy mission has been completed. And in reporting this to you, the people, I speak for the thousands of silent lips, forever stilled among the jungles and the beaches and in the deep waters of the Pacific which marked the way. I speak for the unnamed brave millions homeward bound to take up the challenge of that future which they did so much to salvage from the brink of disaster.
>
> As I look back on the long, tortuous trail from those grim days of Bataan and Corregidor, when an entire world lived in fear, when democracy was on the defensive everywhere, when modern civilization trembled in the balance, I thank a merciful God that He has given us the faith, the courage and the power from which to mould victory. We have known the bitterness of defeat and the exultation of triumph, and from both we have learned there can be no turning back. We must go forward to preserve in peace what we won in war....

We stand in Tokyo today reminiscent of our countryman, Commodore Perry, ninety-two years ago. His purpose was to bring to Japan an era of enlightenment and progress, by lifting the veil of isolation to the friendship, trade, and commerce of the world. But alas the knowledge thereby gained of Western science was forged into an instrument of oppression and human enslavement. Freedom of expression, freedom of action, even freedom of thought were denied through appeal to superstition, and through the application of force. We are committed...to see that the Japanese people are liberated from this condition of slavery. It is my purpose to implement this commitment just as rapidly as the armed forces are demobilized and other essential steps taken to neutralize war potential.

The energy of the Japanese race, if properly directed, will enable expansion vertically rather than horizontally. If the talents of the race are turned into constructive channels, the country can lift itself from its present deplorable state into a position of dignity....

And so, my fellow countrymen, today I report to you that your sons and daughters have served you well and faithfully with the calm, deliberate, determined fighting spirit of the American soldier and sailor, based upon a tradition of historical truth as against the fanaticism of an enemy supported only by mythological fiction. Their spiritual strength and power has brought us through to victory. They are homeward bound—take care of them.

Six days after the surrender ceremony, Douglas made his way to Tokyo, where he would set up his permanent headquarters. As he was being driven along the rubble-strewn highway, he was overcome with the enormity of his task. He now had complete control over eighty million people and the rebuilding of their devastated homes, schools, hospitals, and economy. He had been a military man all his life, and now he was expected to be an economist, political scientist, manufacturing expert, and inspiring Japanese leader. He pulled a field pad out of his pocket and began writing a list of objectives. The list soon read:

First destroy the military power. Punish the criminals. Build the structure of representative government. Modernize the constitution. Hold free elections. Enfranchise the women. Release the political prisoners. Liberate the farmers. Establish a free labor movement. Encourage a free economy. Abolish police oppression. Develop a free and responsible press. Liberalize education. Decentralize the political power. Separate church from state.

It was quite a list, but one Douglas was utterly determined to see carried out.

Chapter 15

Supreme Commander

The building in which Douglas MacArthur set up his new headquarters in Tokyo was called Dai-Ichi, which means "number one" in Japanese. Although the Allied forces had bombed most of the buildings in Tokyo, Dai-Ichi, which had been the offices of an insurance company, had managed to survive the bombing virtually unscathed. Ironically, the building looked out over the very square where during the war the Japanese had said they would publicly hang Douglas if they caught him. From Dai-Ichi, Douglas began his new life as the Supreme Commander for the Allied Powers, or SCAP, as it was soon shortened to.

After Douglas's move to Tokyo, Jean and Arthur flew to Japan to join him. On their arrival Douglas told them that he expected to be in Japan for about five years, as it would take that long to help rebuild the cities and towns. Japan was bitterly cold in winter, and coal production was at one-eighth of what it had been before the war. The textile industry, which had been the mainstay of the prewar Japanese economy, was in a shambles as well. Eighty percent of the textile factories had been converted to making weapons, and most of those factories had been bombed out of existence by Allied planes. Two and a half million homes had been destroyed in the bombing as well, and many people now lived in corrugated iron shacks. Many families had already traded everything they owned for rice. And it was not uncommon for an entire family to be naked, except for one simple cotton kimono that the members of the family took turns wearing when they needed to go out in public.

Not only did Douglas face all of these challenges, but also something was at the heart of Japanese society that had to be totally changed. Until now the Japanese people had believed that their emperor, Hirohito, was a divine figure, more like a god than a man. Tradition said that Emperor Hirohito was the 124th descendent of Emperor Jimmu Tenno, who had ruled Japan in the seventh century B.C. Many myths had grown up around the rule of the emperor. The common people believed that if their eyes met his, even for an instant, they would be struck blind or even die. But most Japanese did not have to worry too much about this because the emperor was seldom seen by the common people, who also had never heard his voice, since he did not speak at public events or on the radio.

The way the Japanese people viewed Emperor Hirohito left Douglas with a big choice to make. On the one hand, the emperor was totally revered by the people. On the other hand, most of the Allies held him responsible for the cruel acts of Japanese soldiers during the war and wanted him executed. Being the SCAP, Douglas had complete power over the fate of the emperor and the military leaders of Japan. He thought long and hard about the dilemma before him, and he finally concluded that any reforms in Japanese culture that were going to be accepted by the people and lead to permanent change were going to have to come with the approval of the emperor. Douglas decided that the best course of action was to be extraordinarily kind to the Japanese people and wait for Emperor Hirohito to realize that the Allied powers were no longer his or the country's enemies.

Of course this policy brought howls of protest from all over the world, particularly from the Russians, who were looking for an opportunity to expand the borders of their country. The Russians argued that they should be allowed to take over the occupation of the northern half of Japan, where they, at least, would see that the Japanese people were punished for what they had done. The British, Australian, and even, to some extent, the United States governments thought this would be a good idea. But Douglas fought it, believing that Japan should have a single, benevolent, occupying power. He told the Russian Consul in Tokyo that he would throw him in jail if one Russian soldier set foot in

Japan. Eventually, in the face of Douglas's resolve, the Russians finally backed down on their demands.

Douglas had to be equally strong with members of the United States government. When Secretary to the Treasury Henry Morgenthau came up with a plan to strip Japan of the little wealth it still possessed, Douglas shot back with a blunt letter.

> If the historian of the future should deem my service worthy of some slight reference, it would be my hope that he would mention me not as a commander engaged in campaigns and battles, even though victorious to American arms, but rather as one whose sacred duty it became, once the guns were silenced, to carry to the land of our vanquished foe the solace and hope and faith of Christian morals.

In keeping with this belief, within weeks of arriving in Japan, Douglas issued orders to lift all restrictions on political, civil, and religious activities. At the same time, a number of the worst war criminals were brought before the courts, and some leaders, including General Masaharu Homma, who had led the Japanese invasion of the Philippines, were executed. Other, lesser figures were allowed to live, as long as they did not hold any position of power in Japan again. In addition, thousands of men who had been wasting away in Japanese prisons for "thinking wrong thoughts" were released from their cells, and the Kempei-Tai, the notorious secret police, was ordered to disband.

A full assessment of the Japanese countryside was soon carried out, and Douglas learned that many of the peasants in remote areas were starving to death. Many of their young men had died fighting in the war, and huge taxes had been levied on the peasants to pay for the war effort. This was Douglas's first opportunity to put his kindness plan into action. He set up soup kitchens and ordered the occupying American soldiers not to eat local food. They could exist on their army rations and leave what was left of the Japanese food supply for the local people. This order made a tremendous impact on the Japanese. They soon realized that Douglas really meant what he said aboard the *Missouri* during the surrender ceremony. The Americans really did want to help Japan get on her feet again rather than hold her down.

Given the food shortage in the country, Douglas cabled Washington, asking for 3.5 million tons of food immediately. The United States government was not impressed with his request, and the Pentagon and State Department stalled on the matter. Douglas was furious. He fired off another cable to Washington. It read in part:

Under the responsibilities of victory the Japanese people are now our prisoners, no less than did the starving men on Bataan become their prisoners when the peninsula fell. As a consequence of the ill treatment, including starvation of Allied prisoners in Japanese hands, we have tried and executed the Japanese officers upon proof of

> responsibility. Can we justify such punitive action if we ourselves, in reversed circumstances but with hostilities at an end, fail to provide the food to sustain life among the Japanese people over whom we now stand guard within the narrow confines of their home island? To cut off Japan's relief supplies in this situation would cause starvation to countless Japanese—and starvation breeds mass unrest, disorder and violence. Give me bread or give me bullets.

Politicians and bureaucrats in Washington got the message and sent the food.

The day after sending the cable to Washington, Douglas overruled an order made by Admiral William Halsey. The admiral had forbidden Japanese fishermen to cross Tokyo Bay because he feared that some of them might want to plant mines on the hulls of the U.S. fleet at anchor there. But Douglas realized that most of the fishermen were simply trying to fend off starvation by fishing, and he struck down the order. Of course, this sent Admiral Halsey into a rage, but it made the Japanese grateful that Douglas trusted them to honor their surrender agreement. Japanese fishing boats were soon bobbing around the American fleet, and not one incident of attempted sabotage to the ships was recorded.

Up to this point Douglas had not yet met Emperor Hirohito, and many of his aides pushed for Douglas to order the emperor to appear before him. Douglas certainly had the power to do this, but he understood that this would cause the emperor and, through him, the entire population to be humiliated, or to lose face, as it was called in Asia. Despite pressure from his aides, he refused to issue such an order.

Soon even Douglas's critics had to agree that he was taking the right track with the emperor. This was because the emperor issued a statement unlike anything any Japanese emperor had ever said before. Emperor Hirohito broadcast a speech over the radio expressing the views of his family. The speech began:

> We stand by the people and we wish always to share with them in their moments of joy and sorrow. The ties between us and our people have always stood upon mutual trust and affection. They do not depend upon mere legends and myth. They are not predicated on the false conception that the emperor is divine and that the Japanese people are superior to other races and fated to rule the world.

Douglas seized upon this new openness and admission from the emperor that he was not a god by sending letters back to the United States asking churches to send as many missionaries as they could provide. He hoped the religious vacuum the emperor had created could be filled with Christian influences.

A week after making his speech on the radio, Emperor Hirohito paid an official visit to Douglas. Dressed in a formal cutaway jacket, striped pants, and top hat, he arrived riding in a gleaming Daimler motorcar. Despite their personal feelings, Douglas had ordered his staff to show the emperor the utmost courtesy as befitting a man of his position. His staff complied, though some of them still thought he should be hanged for his role in the war.

Emperor Hirohito was led into Douglas's office, and after formal introductions he and Douglas and an interpreter sat by the fire and talked for an hour. Douglas reminded the emperor that he had met his father in 1905 while he was aide-de-camp to his own father, who was in Japan inspecting Japanese military bases at the end of the Russo-Japanese War.

The stress of the war was deeply etched into the emperor's face, and his hand shook when he tried to light the cigarette Douglas had offered him. After several minutes of polite conversation, Emperor Hirohito looked at Douglas and declared, "I come to you, General MacArthur, to offer myself to the judgement of the powers you represent as the one to bear sole responsibility for every political and military decision made and action taken by my people in the conduct of war."

Douglas was deeply touched by this. Yes, the emperor was ultimately responsible for the actions of Japan during the war. But the emperor had no idea that Douglas had convinced the Allies not to arrest and punish him. As far as Emperor Hirohito was aware, in taking responsibility in this way for the actions of his people, he was facing certain execution. Douglas was amazed by the man's courageousness. And one thing Douglas MacArthur liked was a courageous man. As a result, Emperor Hirohito made many more visits to Douglas. The two men talked about a wide range of topics on these visits, and Douglas was particularly impressed with the emperor's grasp of democracy and how it could revolutionize his country.

No relationship like this with the emperor had ever occurred before, and the Japanese people were stunned. Once they recovered, they realized that things could never be the way they had been before—they no longer had a divine leader, and they were not destined to rule the world as an invincible power. As a result they took a good look at themselves and saw a very poor country that had waged a brave but ultimately futile war against the Western world. Now they wanted to be a part of that Western world. The one thing that stopped them was their lack of natural resources. But instead of attempting to take over the countries that had the resources they needed and wanted, they now understood that they had to manufacture products that other countries wanted and peacefully trade them for the resources they needed.

The challenges they faced in doing this were huge. But with the emperor's encouragement and Douglas's foresight, the foundations of an entirely new Japan began to emerge.

The Japanese people came to love and trust Douglas MacArthur completely. Every day when he returned home for lunch, a crowd was waiting at the gate for him. Douglas always had his chauffeur drive the same route home, and soon the streets they drove along became so overcrowded that permanent markings had to be made on the pavement delineating where spectators could stand to get a glimpse of their Supreme Commander. Some of Douglas's aides questioned his judgement in using the same route and driving so slowly. They argued that he was a perfect target for those ex-military men who hated him and might try to assassinate him. Indeed, a plot to throw hand grenades at his car while it passed by was uncovered, but Douglas would not take any extra precautions. He told his aides, "In the Orient, the man who shows no fear is master. I count on the Japanese people to protect me."

Once, on his way back to his office, Douglas stepped into the elevator after a carpenter. When the carpenter realized that he was standing next to Douglas MacArthur, he bowed deeply and began backing out of the elevator. Douglas held up his hand. "Please stay," he said.

A week later Douglas received a letter from the carpenter. It read, "I am a humble Japanese carpenter who last week you not only permitted but insisted ride with you in the same elevator. I have reflected on this act of courtesy for a whole week, and I realize that no Japanese general would have done as you did."

Soon newspapers got ahold of the story, and numerous articles were written about it. These were followed by a one-act play on the event and an oil painting depicting Douglas motioning to the carpenter. This painting became enormously popular, and copies of it hung in millions of Japanese homes. It symbolized the new Japan—friendly, outward looking, and democratic.

On Wednesday, April 10, 1946, the first full and democratic elections ever held in Japan took place. An array of issues were debated, and the quality of candidates standing for election was stunning. Douglas encouraged the people not only to debate the issues but also to go and vote. On election day three-quarters of those eligible to vote went to the ballot box to have their say regarding the direction of the new Japan. The people voted into office forty-nine farmers, thirteen doctors, thirty-two teachers, and twenty-two authors. The group included thirty-eight women, a reflection of the fact that Douglas had insisted on giving women the right to vote.

Now that there was a democratically elected assembly, or Diet, as it was called, Douglas set out a list of things he expected the members of the Diet to accomplish. The first thing on the list was making women equal in all areas of life. Before the war, fathers had arranged their daughters' marriages, and the daughters had no right to refuse to go through with the ceremony. In addition, there were no colleges for women, and it was nearly impossible for a woman to divorce her husband, while it was a simple matter for a man to divorce his wife.

Echoes of his mother's sense of justice reverberated in Douglas as he called for this major reform. Women and men were now to be treated exactly the same under the law—if it was good enough for one, it was good enough for the other. This led to a tremendous surge in activity among women. Twenty-six universities were opened for women, and women soon found seats on city councils and in town assemblies. In Tokyo itself, two thousand women were admitted into the police force. This move sent shock waves through Japan and into the rest of Asia. Under the "MacArthur Constitution" women were actually given authority over men!

As 1946 rolled on and then 1947 and 1948, Japan continued her steady climb toward a more open society. Douglas was extremely pleased with the way things were going. What he was not pleased about was what was happening on his back doorstep in China. A growing Communist movement in that country was slowly taking control of large portions of countryside. And to Douglas's dismay, the West seemed impotent to do anything about it. Finally, on October 1, 1949, the Chinese Communist Party under the leadership of Mao Zedong took complete control of China and declared the establishment of the People's Republic of China.

Having a huge Communist state to the west put tremendous pressure on the Japanese, and Douglas feared that other parts of Asia would be drawn into the Communist sphere. Already this had happened in Korea. At the end of the war, when the Japanese left the Korean peninsula, which they had occupied for thirty-five years, Korea was divided into two zones. Soviet troops would occupy the northern half of the peninsula above the thirty-eighth parallel, and American troops would occupy the south. Initially the Soviets and the Americans had cooperated as they sought some way to unify the two halves into one country. But then in 1947 the Soviet Union had balked at holding United Nations–sanctioned elections in the North, and a stalemate developed between North and South Korea. In 1948 Korea was formally divided between two regimes, with the Democratic People's Republic in the North and the Republic of Korea in the South.

Now that China was a Communist nation, it began to eye Korea and saw the benefits of the peninsula's being completely in Communist hands. So along with the Soviets, China began to encourage Kim Il Sung, North Korea's premier, to move south and conquer the Republic of Korea. Tensions began to mount on the Korean peninsula, and Douglas began to fear what might happen next.

The thing Douglas feared most occurred early one summer Sunday morning. It was June 25, 1950, and the telephone beside his bed rang. Douglas picked up the receiver and listened as a voice on the other end said, "General, I am sorry to disturb you at this early hour, but we have just received a dispatch from Seoul, advising that the North Koreans have struck in strength across the thirty-eighth parallel at four o'clock this morning."

"Thank you for the information," Douglas said as he climbed out of bed and pulled on his robe.

He walked to the living room and paced the floor. He had a terrible sense of history repeating itself. Nine years before he had been in bed in the early morning when the phone rang and an aide informed him that the Japanese had bombed Pearl Harbor. Now, it seemed, another war was breaking out, and seventy-year-old General Douglas MacArthur wondered what role his country would have him play this time around.

Chapter 16

Korea

It was not until the following morning that Douglas received instructions from President Truman regarding what to do. The message was sent by the latest communication tool, the teleconn, which consisted of two typewriters and two television screens. The message that appeared on Douglas's screen was clear. The president gave him the command of all United States forces in Asia and, along with that, the new title of Commander in Chief, Far East, or CINCFE for short. Douglas's orders were to evacuate the two thousand Americans in South Korea. Next, Douglas was to support the South Koreans in their bid to repulse the North Koreans from their land. To do this, Douglas was permitted to use ships and planes over South Korean airspace, but he was not to commit any ground troops to the action. The South Koreans were expected to do the combat on land.

Douglas was surprised when he read the message. President Truman appeared to be acting without the approval of Congress. Douglas also was concerned that the small group of Pentagon advisers the president was relying upon for guidance had little experience in Asia and were sure to make mistakes. And while the war in Korea was already under way and Americans were committed to air and sea raids, Douglas found that he was loath to preside over more bloodshed in his lifetime.

But there was a job to be done, and the president had called on him to do it. Within an hour of receiving the message from Washington, Douglas had ships headed for the South Korean port of Inchon and airplanes on their way to Seoul to pick up American citizens. The operation went off without a hitch, and although the Americans encountered North Korean planes, not a single life was lost in the evacuation.

With all nonessential American personnel now out of Korea, Douglas settled down to monitor the fighting. He did not like what he read over the teleconn. The South Koreans seemed hopelessly outnumbered. Most estimates put their number at one hundred thousand soldiers, while the North Koreans fielded an army of two hundred thousand. And that was not the worst of it. The South Korean army, which had been trained by the Americans, was a peacekeeping force. It had few weapons larger than a rifle and was lightly trained. By contrast, the

Chinese had trained the North Koreans in aggressive warfare techniques, and the North Koreans were armed with tanks and heavy artillery. It was an uneven show of strength, one that Douglas was not sure could be evened up unless the United States committed ground troops.

Finally Douglas decided that there was only one way to know for sure what exactly was happening on the ground in Korea, and that was to inspect the battlefield himself. Douglas ordered his aircraft, named the *Bataan,* to be readied for a flight to South Korea. When the plane took off early Thursday morning, the fifth day of the war, he had little idea of which airstrips he could still land at, but he went anyway. One way or another, he was determined to set foot on the Korean peninsula and assess the situation.

The *Bataan* finally set down at Suwon, a small airfield twenty miles south of Seoul, where the small group of American military officers in the country advising the South Korean army met Douglas. Within minutes Douglas had climbed into a black Dodge motorcar, and escorted by an entourage of Jeeps, they headed north toward the Han River, which ran through Seoul. As they made their way along, the road was clogged by decimated and retreating South Korean soldiers and by disheveled refugees fleeing the North Korean advance.

As they got closer to Seoul, black columns of smoke rose from the city, which the North Koreans had just captured. As they approached the Han River, the Dodge pulled to the side of the road beside a grassy knoll. Douglas climbed to the top of the rise, and with his corncob pipe jutting from his mouth, he peered out through his field glasses. The sight that greeted Douglas was one of utter destruction. The bridges across the Han River into Seoul were destroyed, the river flowed with bodies, and the flames rising from Seoul were now clearly visible. North Korean planes and artillery fire whizzed overhead. After twenty minutes of standing on top of the knoll viewing the scene, Douglas climbed back into the Dodge, and the group headed back to Suwon, from where Douglas would depart.

As Douglas sat on the plane heading for Tokyo, he pulled out a yellow pad and pencil and composed a report to President Truman. In it he explained that he was not sure the South Koreans could push back the North Koreans unless he was authorized to use U.S. ground troops. And such authorization would have to come quickly, before it was too late.

When he got back to his office in Tokyo, Douglas had the report teleconned to the Pentagon. By the following morning Douglas had his reply. President Truman had authorized him to send American ground troops into Korea, as well as conduct air raids and use the navy to blockade the entire Korean coastline. In less than twenty-four hours the first battalions of soldiers were climbing aboard aircraft for the flight from Japan's northern islands to Pusan in southeastern Korea. Douglas did not like to enter a war this way, with a small number of troops and no time to plan his strategy, but he felt he had little choice. If he delayed, the North Koreans would take over the entire Korean peninsula.

The first two U.S. divisions to arrive in South Korea were outnumbered by their enemy twenty to one. To make matters even worse, over 80 percent of the American troops were young and had never fought in a war before. The situation was hopeless. Many of these young men surrendered as North Korea's Soviet-supplied tanks barreled down upon them. But they soon found out that they would have been better off fighting to the death. The North Koreans took few prisoners, preferring to bayonet the surrendering Americans to death on the field of battle.

When Douglas learned what had happened, he knew he had to do something to fool the North Koreans into thinking there were many more battalions of soldiers arriving daily. He started by instituting a buddy system by which each American soldier was teamed with a South Korean fighter, doubling the fighting power of the American forces.

Douglas also sent parts of two battalions of infantry to the peninsula, where they put up a gallant fight before being destroyed. Just as he had hoped, the small force seemed to confuse the North Koreans. So instead of continuing on with their relentless push to capture Pusan at the south of the Korean peninsula, they decided to stop their advance and deploy heavy artillery. This decision gave Douglas what he needed—ten days to bring in more troops, who quickly formed a battle line to confront the North Koreans.

Slowly the American troops and their South Korean partners got the upper hand. And with the arrival of U.S. tanks and heavy weapons, in August they were finally able to stop the North Koreans' advance at Taegu, where both sides dug into their positions.

Soon fresh troops directly from the United States arrived to join the fight. By now the United Nations had officially sanctioned the war, and British troops from Hong Kong began arriving, as did troops from France, Turkey, the Netherlands, and the Philippines. Smaller military units arrived from thirteen other United Nations member countries.

As the weather began to get colder, there were many skirmishes at the frontline, but neither side had the complete upper hand. The Americans lost troops but were able to replace them quickly. The North Koreans did so too. Soon Douglas and the rest of the world were asking, *What happens next?*

Finally Douglas decided that the UN troops needed to advance and start winning territory back from the North Koreans. He thought the South Korean capital city of Seoul would be a great place to begin. To do this he hatched perhaps the most daring campaign of his military career—an invasion of the Port of Inchon.

On the night of September 14, 1950, a fleet of 261 ships from seven nations approached Flying Fish Channel at the entrance to Inchon Harbor. The channel lights still blazed, and it was obvious that the North Koreans had not spotted the approaching fleet.

As dawn broke the following morning, Douglas was standing on the bridge of the *Mount McKinley* as the ship's guns opened fire on Wolmi-do, the site of a fort that guarded the harbor. The gunfire smashed into the fort, and at 8:00 AM Douglas received word that U.S. marines had captured the fort.

As Wolmi-do was being captured, other ships had moved up the channel and into the harbor, where more marines began going ashore. But this was no easy task. The tide in Inchon Harbor rose and fell thirty-two feet, exposing vast, impassable mud flats at low tide. As a result, those marines going ashore in the first wave at dawn would have to wait until dusk, when the tide would be high enough again for the amphibious landing to continue. To make matters worse, there was no beach at Inchon on which to land, only rocks and a seawall. In addition, the marines were landing in the middle of a city, where the North Koreans could rain down gunfire on them from the surrounding buildings. For all these reasons it was the most unlikely place to make such a landing. And that was why Douglas had chosen the place. The element of surprise would be on his side.

And so it was. The North Koreans seemed to be completely stunned by the attack, and taking Inchon proved to be not nearly as difficult as everyone had thought it would be. The second wave of marines went ashore on the high tide at dusk, and by the time Douglas finally went ashore the following morning, the marines had pushed three miles inland from their beachhead. The following day they had captured Kimpo Airfield on the outskirts of Seoul, and American planes began using it to bring in fresh supplies and reinforcements.

Three days after the landing at Inchon, UN forces in the south crossed the Naktong River and began pushing forward. Surprised, and with their supply lines cut, the North Koreans began to fall back. Fifteen days after the daring raid on Inchon, the North Koreans had been pushed all the way back to the thirty-eighth parallel. They were back at the place they had started from.

Douglas's next order from the Pentagon was very vague. He was ordered to extend his operations north of the parallel and to make plans for the occupation of North Korea, under one condition: that these moves did not provoke China or Russia to step up its aid to North Korea, thus causing a third world war.

A United Nations resolution passed on October 4 gave Douglas approval to move north of the thirty-eighth parallel, with the goal of reunifying Korea into one country.

Sixteen days later Douglas's troops had captured Pyongyang, the North Korean capital. Douglas was delighted at the rapid advance, and he saw no reason why his forces should not push all the way to the northern border with Manchuria. However, before he could do this, the ground rules for the fight were changed. The Pentagon issued new orders that said he was not to pursue Chinese airplanes over the Manchurian border, nor was he allowed to bomb strategic North Korean sites, including hydroelectric plants, bridges, and the huge supply depot at Racin in the northeastern corner of Korea, through which the Soviet Union forwarded supplies to the North Koreans.

These new orders frustrated Douglas more than any other military strategy he had ever had to work under. In his opinion he could declare victory and have his men home in time for Thanksgiving dinner if only he would be allowed to fight the way he liked to fight. Instead of defeating the North Koreans, President Truman seemed to think it was good enough just to contain them.

The battles continued, with Douglas doing his best to follow the new ground rules. But it was difficult not being able to destroy the enemy's supply dumps and infrastructure.

As the fighting went on, Douglas noticed many occasions when the enemy seemed to predict exactly what he was going to do next. This was very baffling to him, and it would be years before he learned that three high-ranking members of the British embassy in Washington were in fact Communist agents. Since the war in Korea was a joint operation, the Pentagon was passing copies of Douglas's most sensitive battle plans to the embassy to be forwarded on to the British government. The agents at the British embassy were also sending copies of the plans to the Soviet Union, who in turn shared them with China and North Korea. Because of this, Douglas began to lose the one advantage he had always relied on—surprise.

The Chinese, however, had a mammoth surprise in store for the United Nations troops. On November 27 seven Chinese Communist field armies attacked the UN forces. Douglas realized they had built themselves up at the border under cover of darkness. The situation became alarming. Douglas teleconned the Pentagon asking for thirty-three thousand more troops. He was astonished and angered when his request was denied. The Pentagon said that it had to keep troops in reserve and ready to go to Europe in case the Soviet Union took advantage of the situation and started a war there. The Joint Chiefs of Staff sent Douglas a message that read, "We believe North Korea is not the place to fight a major war."

In Douglas's opinion a major war was already well under way there. Discouraged and disgusted, Douglas withdrew 105,000 soldiers and 100,000 refugees from north of the thirty-eighth parallel to avoid their being captured by Chinese army units. Still, Douglas tried hard to think of another way forward. On December 30 he proposed a plan to blockade the east coast of China, bomb China's industrial centers from the air, and reinforce the United Nations troops in Korea. The Pentagon turned his plan down, giving the same reason about not wanting to start a world war.

Meanwhile Douglas was concerned that if the United Nations was not aggressive against the Chinese, the Chinese would not stop until they conquered South Korea and then much of Asia. His worst fears were confirmed when on January 4, 1951, Chinese forces swooped down across the thirty-eighth parallel and recaptured Seoul.

Once again Douglas came up with a plan. This time he planned to retake Seoul, fight the Chinese back across the Yalu River into Manchuria, and then make the south bank of the Yalu radioactive so that no one could cross from China into Korea. It was a bold and ambitious plan, and Douglas sent a copy of it to House Minority Leader Joseph Martin, along with the admonition, "There is no substitute for victory."

Representative Martin released Douglas's letter to the press, and a hailstorm of protest followed. Many Americans felt that Douglas was being disloyal, or even insubordinate, to the president by publicly advocating his own plan. President Truman, the Joint Chiefs of Staff, and the Secretaries of State and Defense were alarmed that Douglas had made an unauthorized public statement about United States policy that contradicted the administration's strategy, especially since they had ordered him not to do so and had informed him that the United Nations was preparing for peace negotiations with the Chinese.

Douglas waited for the clamor to die down, but it did not. On April 11, 1951, Douglas was at his home in Tokyo finishing lunch. Jean was there, along with a few guests. Douglas was in the middle of telling a story when he noticed his aide Colonel Sidney Huff beckon Jean to the door. Jean came back a moment later pale and shaken.

When Douglas finished what he was saying, Jean leaned over and whispered in his ear. "Sid says he just heard on the radio that President Truman has relieved you of all command," she told him.

Douglas paused for a moment to take in the news. Then he reached for his wife's hand. "Jeannie," he said, "we're going home at last."

Chapter 17

What Greater Honor

News that Douglas MacArthur had been relieved of command traveled fast. Before the day was over, Japan's newspapers were echoing the disbelief of the nation. Emperor Hirohito came to visit Douglas. Tears streamed down his face as he thanked Douglas for his service to the Japanese people, not as a conqueror but as their reformer. The *Nippon Times* wrote that "the good wishes of eighty-three million Japanese people" would go with him and that mere words could never describe adequately all that he had meant to the nation. Another newspaper wrote of Douglas as a "noble political missionary. What he gave us was not material aid and democratic reform alone, but a new way of life, the freedom and dignity of the individual."

The MacArthurs did not want to stay in Japan any longer than was necessary to pack their belongings, and so on April 16, 1951, Douglas, Jean, thirteen-year-old Arthur, and Ah Cheu left their home at the American embassy for the last time.

Day had just broken as they climbed into the limousine and began the drive to Atsugi Air Force Base in Yokohama, the same air base Douglas had arrived at five and a half years before to accept Japan's formal surrender. Then, Douglas's aides had feared he might be assassinated on his arrival. Now, Douglas was leaving from the same spot as the most popular person in Japan.

As the limousine drove along, Douglas was moved to tears at the sight of nearly a quarter of a million Japanese people—farmers, laundresses, laborers—who lined the route. Many of them had stood all night to be in the front row of spectators to catch one last glimpse of their supreme commander. They waved Japanese and American flags and shouted, "Sayonara. We love you," as the limousine passed. Douglas had come to love them in his own way, too.

As they drove along, Douglas thought about the events of the past few days. He could hardly believe the swiftness with which he had been removed from command, and that he'd had to hear of it not from the Pentagon but from the radio like everyone else. Given these circumstances, he knew that some of his supporters in Washington were calling on Congress to launch an inquiry into his dismissal.

On the flight from Japan to Hawaii, Douglas spent most of his time writing a speech, which he was to deliver to a joint session of Congress.

There was no way that Douglas or anyone else could have predicted the crowd that awaited him at Hickam Field in Honolulu, when the *Bataan*, his Lockheed Constellation airplane, touched down to refuel. Over one hundred thousand cheering people waited behind barricades to yell their support and best wishes to Douglas and his family.

This made Douglas glad that he had planned things so they would arrive in San Francisco at eight thirty in the evening, a time he hoped would discourage a crowd from forming to greet him.

As the lights of San Francisco shimmered in the distance, Douglas drew Arthur to the window. "Well, my boy, we are home," he said.

It was a home that Arthur had never seen before. And indeed, it was the first time in sixteen years that Douglas had been "home" himself.

The *Bataan* touched down safely in San Francisco, and Douglas thanked the pilot for a smooth flight. When the door to the airplane was opened, Douglas stepped out onto the metal stairway that led to the tarmac. Lights suddenly flashed in his face, and cannons boomed overhead. Between the thunder of the cannon booms, an army band belted out a tune. As Douglas adjusted to the bright lights, ten thousand spectators surged over the police lines and ran toward the *Bataan*. Women sobbed and men saluted as Douglas led his family through the crowd to the awaiting limousine. But the ordeal was not over yet. Reporters would later estimate that over a half million San Franciscans lined the streets to the St. Francis Hotel, where the MacArthur family was to stay.

It took the motorcade two hours to creep along the crowded route, and the MacArthurs were exhausted by the time they arrived in their hotel suite. But they were not too exhausted to turn the knob on the box that sat in the corner. It was a television set, and none of them had ever seen one before. They called for room service, and Arthur ordered a milkshake, an item he had read about in American magazines but had never experienced for himself.

The next day another crowd of a half million people gathered to see Douglas reboard the *Bataan* for the flight to Washington, D.C.

The family arrived at Washington National Airport at midnight, where another massive crowd awaited them. It took Douglas a quarter of an hour to fight his way to the limousine. Officials who had come to welcome him to Washington were knocked off their feet in the crush. The only people who dressed for the pandemonium that erupted were the Washington correspondents, who had worn football helmets.

Finally, at about 2:00 AM, the MacArthur family made it to their hotel room. Douglas tucked his wife and son into bed and then spent another hour or so polishing the speech he was to deliver to a joint session of Congress at noon that day. When he was satisfied that he had covered everything he wanted to cover in the speech, Douglas slept for a few hours. When daylight came, he was up again, polishing the speech still more. By now he had learned that the speech was to be broadcast across the United States. So besides the members of Congress, about thirty million Americans were expected to tune in and listen to him speak.

As he worked on the speech, Douglas hoped that the members of Congress would pay attention. They certainly did. When the gathered assembly quieted down, Douglas began. "Mr. President, Mr. Speaker, distinguished Members of Congress. I stand on this rostrum with a sense of deep humility and great pride.... I address you with neither rancor nor bitterness in the fading twilight of life with but one purpose in mind: to serve my country."

The chamber went wild, stomping the floor and whistling. When order was restored, Douglas spoke for several minutes about what he believed to be the growing menace of China. He told the members of Congress that he could see a time when China would attack Indochina and Tibet and that the best way to stop this from happening was for the United Nations to take aggressive steps to stop the Communist tide. He argued that containing China would never solve the problems, saying, "Once war is forced upon us, there is no alternative than to apply every available means to bring it to a swift end. War's very object is victory—not prolonged indecision. In war, indeed, there can be no substitute for victory."

There was another standing ovation. Douglas turned over the last page of his speech and read: "I am closing my fifty-two years of military service. When I joined the army even before the turn of the century, it was the fulfillment of all my boyish hopes and dreams. The world has turned over many times since I took the oath on the plain at West Point, and the hopes and dreams have long vanished. But I still remember the refrain of one of the most popular barrack ballads of that day, which proclaimed most proudly that 'old soldiers never die; they just fade away.' And like the old soldier in that ballad, I now close my military career and just fade away— an old soldier who tried to do his duty as God gave him the light to see that duty. Goodbye."

The idea that Douglas MacArthur would fade away was soon dropped. His speech had caused a sensation. Members of Congress were declaring that it was as if they had heard St. Paul the apostle talking to them that day, and some even suggested it was more like God talking to Moses on the mountaintop! When Douglas emerged into the sunlight after giving his speech, a half million Washingtonians were waiting for him. His motorcade carried him down Pennsylvania Avenue while a squadron of air force jets swooped low over the city.

From Washington Douglas was driven on to New York City, where he transferred to an open-topped Chrysler for a ticker tape parade through Manhattan. The twenty-mile route of the parade took nearly seven hours to cover, as several million spectators craned their necks for a glimpse of their hero. Douglas ordered that the car be stopped outside St. Patrick's Cathedral so that he could shake the hand of Francis Joseph Cardinal Spellman, archbishop of New York and vicar of the United States Armed Forces, and again at City Hall to address the sixty thousand people who had gathered there.

It was the largest parade New York had ever seen, and when it was over 2,859 tons of ticker tape were swept from Manhattan's streets.

The MacArthurs had decided to make their home in Manhattan, and Suite 37A at the Waldorf Astoria Hotel had been prepared for them to move into. When they arrived at the hotel, mail for Douglas was piling up by the sackful. Over 150,000 letters and 20,000 telegrams congratulating Douglas on his long and distinguished career awaited him that first day.

That spring, as Douglas had anticipated, members of the Joint Committee on Armed Forces and Foreign Relations of the United States Senate conducted an inquiry into his dismissal. They concluded that President Truman had acted within his Constitutional powers when removing Douglas from command, but they didn't all believe that Douglas's actions had justified his removal.

Regardless of the startling end to Douglas's command in the Far East, Americans, including President Truman, seemed to agree that Douglas's decades of service had been exceptional, securing him a permanent place of honor in the life of the nation. Accordingly, life was hectic in the MacArthur household. Five-star generals cannot retire, and although they are relieved of command, they are given a government allowance to maintain their own staff and transportation. Douglas could have kept the *Bataan* as his own personal airplane, but he decided to release it back to the army. With troops still in Korea, he figured that they needed it more than he did.

During his first eighteen months back in the United States, Douglas spoke in countless legion halls, universities, and Republican party rallies. By 1952 his name was being bandied around as a possible presidential candidate. Douglas was ready for a new challenge, and he actively pursued the nomination. However, his old chief of staff Dwight Eisenhower won the nomination, thus ending Douglas's experiment with elected office.

Although he was now seventy-two years old, Douglas was not ready to "fade away," as he had suggested he might. Instead he accepted the position of board chairman for the Remington Rand Corporation, best known for its pioneering work in computers. He threw himself into his new job, dividing his time between corporate offices in Bridgeport and Norwalk, Connecticut, and the Waldorf Astoria.

The stalemate between North and South Korea continued, and Douglas despaired over America's lost opportunity. He was quoted by newspapers as saying, "A great nation that enters upon war and does not see it through to victory must ultimately suffer all the consequences of defeat. That is what happened to us in Korea. With victory within our grasp and without the use of the atom bomb, which we needed no more than against Japan, we failed to see it through. Had we done so, we would have destroyed Red China's capability of waging modern war for a generation to come."

The City of Los Angeles marked Douglas's birthday with a statue in his honor. On the statue was carved his personal credo, "Battles are not won by arms alone. There must exist above all else a spiritual impulse—a will to victory. In war there can be no substitute for victory."

Throughout this time not a day went by when Douglas did not think about the Far East, and so when he was invited to attend the fifteenth anniversary of Philippine independence, he jumped at the chance. He set off in July 1961 with Jean and twenty-three-year-old Arthur at his side. Arthur had just graduated from Columbia University and was preparing for a musical career. Much to his father's initial disappointment, he had chosen not to continue in the long military line he descended from.

Suddenly it felt like forty years had dropped away as Douglas stood in Luneta Park beside Manila Bay. A million people surged around him, the largest crowd ever to assemble in the Philippines. Over the next ten days Douglas visited all of the major battle sites, including Corregidor island, Lingayen, and the Bataan peninsula. So much had changed, yet so much remained just the way he remembered it.

Douglas was asked to address the Philippine legislature, and for the first time he was so overcome while making a speech that he could barely continue. The ghosts of so many men haunted him as he said, "My thoughts go back to those men who went with us to their last campaign. I do not know the dignity of their birth, but I do know the glory of their death. Their flags will wave again only in the evening of our memory. Under white crosses, in chambered temples of silence the dust of their dauntless valor rests—waiting, waiting in the chancellery of heaven, and the final reckoning of judgement day."

More memories were rekindled for Douglas when, back in the United States, he was invited to receive the Sylvanus Thayer Award for distinguished service to the nation. The award was presented to him in a ceremony at West Point in May 1962. This time Douglas did not write a speech. He stood and spoke from his heart to the young cadets, saying:

> The shadows are lengthening for me. The twilight is here. My days have vanished— tone and tint. They have gone glimmering through the dreams of things that were. Their memory is one of wondrous beauty, watered by tears and coaxed and caressed by the smiles of yesterday. I listen vainly, but with thirsty ear, for the witching melody of faint bugles blowing reveille, of far drums beating the long roll.
>
> In my dreams I hear again the crash of guns, the rattle of musketry, the strange, mournful mutter of the battlefield. But in the evening of my memory always I come back to West Point. Always there echoes and re-echoes: Duty, honor, country.
>
> Today marks my final roll call with you. But I want you to know that when I cross the river, my last conscious thoughts will be of the corps, and the corps and the corps.
>
> I bid you farewell.

Not much was left undone in Douglas MacArthur's life, except for one large project. For fifty years he had collected army papers with the thought that one day he might write his memoirs. Now, with his public speaking behind him, Douglas decided to make a start. In typical fashion he worked ceaselessly, writing every word himself on a series of yellow lined pads. By the time he finished, he had written 220,000 words. Time-Life bought the manuscript and the rights to make a motion picture based on it for one million dollars.

The book was the last great task Douglas MacArthur undertook, and it was published under the title *Reminiscences.* Once it was finished, Douglas's health began to fail. The man who had gone for thirty years without a single day off for sickness suddenly found himself at the army's Walter Reed Medical Center. In March 1964 photographers snapped photos of eighty-four-year-old Douglas hobbling into Walter Reed on the arm of the surgeon general.

Initially the news was hopeful. Douglas had a malfunctioning gallbladder that was successfully removed. However, complications developed, and a second surgery was performed and then a third. Douglas never regained consciousness after the third operation. The lengthening shadows he had talked about at West Point two years before had finally engulfed him.

At 2:39 PM on Sunday, April 5, 1964, the flags flying over Walter Reed Medical Center were lowered to half-staff. The five-star general in their midst was dead.

The country rallied upon hearing news of Douglas's death. His casket was placed in the rotunda of the Capitol Building in Washington, the temporary resting place of presidents. Behind the coffin was a huge poster that read: "Douglas MacArthur— General of the Army." Around the inside of the rotunda were listed the battles Douglas had fought in; the name Corregidor lay directly at the head of the casket. Five men representing the five services, the army, navy, marine corps, coast guard, and the air force, guarded the casket.

On Saturday, April 11, the casket was escorted from the rotunda in a procession of six horses, with a seventh riderless horse, signifying a fallen soldier. The casket was flown to the Naval Air Station in Norfolk, Virginia, where the funeral service was held at St. Paul's Episcopal Church. Douglas's body was then entombed at Norfolk's 114-year-old courthouse.

After his funeral many people were surprised to learn that Douglas MacArthur had been buried in his oldest and most worn suntan, an everyday summer uniform, with no medals or ribbons pinned to his breast. Before his death Douglas had explained his wishes. "I suppose, in a way, this [everyday uniform] has become part of my soul. It is a symbol of my life. Whatever I've done that really matters, I've done wearing it. When the time comes, it will be these that I journey forth in. What greater honor could come to an American and a soldier?"

What greater honor indeed?

———————————————————— *Bibliography*

Blair, Clay, Jr. *MacArthur.* Pocket Books, 1977.

Considine, Bob. *General Douglas MacArthur.* Gold Medal Books, 1964.

Editors of the *Army Times. The Banners and the Glory: The Story of General Douglas MacArthur.* G. P. Putnam, 1965.

Hunt, Frazier. *The Untold Story of Douglas MacArthur.* Signet Books, 1954.

MacArthur, Douglas. *Reminiscences.* McGraw-Hill, 1964.

Manchester, William. *American Caesar.* Little, Brown, 1978.

Janet and Geoff Benge are a husband and wife writing team with more than twenty years of writing experience. Janet is a former elementary school teacher. Geoff holds a degree in history. Together they have a passion to make history come alive for a new generation of readers.

Originally from New Zealand, the Benges make their home in the Orlando, Florida, area.